P9-CEX-670

I LIKE YOU JUST THE WAY I AM

I LIKE YOU JUST THE WAY I AM

Stories About Me and Some Other People

Jenny Mollen

St. Martin's Press New York

Printed in the United States of America. For information, address St. Martin's Press, 175 Fifth Avenue, New York, N.Y. 10010.

Some of these stories appeared in revised and abbreviated form in *Playboy*'s TheSmokingJacket.com.

Photograph of painting on page 57 by Eoin McShane

www.stmartins.com

Design by Patrice Sheridon

LIBRARY OF CONGRESS CATALOGING-IN-PUBLICATION DATA

Mollen, Jenny, 1979–
I like you just the way I am : stories about me and some other people / Jenny Mollen. — First edition.
p. cm.
ISBN 978-1-250-04168-5 (hardcover)
ISBN 978-1-4668-3858-1 (e-book)
1. Mollen, Jenny—Anecdotes. 2. Actors—United States—Anecdotes. I. Title.
PN2287 .M655A3 2014
792.02'8092—dc23

2014008150

First Edition: June 2014

10 9 8 7 6 5 4 3 2 1

"I'm just looking for a girl who isn't drama."

–MY HUSBAND, THE FIRST NIGHT WE MET.

(I love you)

Contents

Author's Note

The stories you are about to read are basically true. Though I tried to do my best in depicting the events as I remembered them, there are exaggerations, some characters are composites, and some time periods are condensed. The only thing I'm sure of with complete certainty is that I was really thin and cute the whole time I was writing this.

Introduction

Hi, I'm Jenny Mollen, an actress and writer living in Los Angeles. I'm also a wife, married to a famous guy, which is infinitely annoying, because all the free stuff he gets never comes in my size. Sometimes I wish I'd married Ellen.

Now, I'm self aware enough to know that underneath my charming exterior, I'm an insecure mess of a person who hates herself. But despite all that, it's still pretty great being me. Why? Because I don't pretend I'm *not* crazy. You guys, I am! But so are you! "Crazy" is just a word boring people use to describe fun people. And I am really, really fun!

What you're about to read is a collection of stories about my life. It's a book about not doing the right thing. Yes, it's about me (not doing the right thing), but it is also a book about women, all of whom come in two types: those who are totally batshit crazy, and those who are liars. It's a book about acting on impulses, plotting elaborate hoaxes, and refusing to acknowledge boundaries in any form. Because why not? You're already doing it secretly anyway. And reading your ex's horoscope every week isn't going to help you control his life. No, you need to hide in his bushes, break into his e-mail, or kidnap his dog if you want to effect any real change.

We are a generation of females that never had to burn our bras, get a back-alley Mexican boob job, or bleed into a make-shift cloth diaper because tampons weren't invented. Our generation is fighting for something different: honesty. Decorum went out the window when Madonna made the movie *Truth or Dare,* ladies. We don't need to be perfect. We need to be real.

This is my mission statement, my manifesto, and my plea to women everywhere: Indulge your inner sociopath. People are judging you anyway. That's what people do. I'm judging you right now for reading this book. There is zero reason to be ashamed of announcing and acting upon your real feelings.

Life is too short for bullshit. I'm thirty-three, and my tits drop about half an inch a year. In other words, it's all downhill from here. Someday very soon, ladies, we are going to be whatever fetish comes after "cougar," unable to wear shirts without sleeves, and full of cell phone cancer. It is our obligation to live lives that convince our children not to ship us off to retirement homes because we are still kind of entertaining to have at parties. This book is utterly who I am when I am not trying to impress or protect someone's feelings. It is my hope that you read it and become better acquainted with who you really are and what you really want. Which, let's be honest, is most likely someone else's e-mail password.

I LIKE YOU JUST THE WAY I AM

1.

Behind Every Crazy Woman, There's an Even More Batshit Mother

My mom was always more of a friend than an authority figure. But not like a laid-back friend who comes over to watch *Homeland*—more like an annoying friend who comes over with two dudes you don't know and starts doing body shots off your sleeping roommate at 3 A.M. on a Wednesday.

Everyone's mom is fucking crazy to some degree, and my mom is no different. Except that she's *completely* different because she is infinitely crazier than your mom. She is a product of Ashland, Oregon, in the 1960s, a reaction to a generation of Betty Homemakers and Goody Two-Shoes, and a man-eater with a serious penchant for partying. In her youth, my mom looked like a real-life Barbie. She has blond hair, one green eye and one blue eye, and tits that I inherited only after surgery. Though she always emphasized brains over beauty—by talking shit about any woman who didn't make her own money and own at least one copy of *Jonathan Livingston Seagull*—my mom's identity was heavily wrapped up in her physical appearance, and attention from the opposite sex was a prize I could never compete with. After dissecting her psychologically over the years, I feel I understand why she never stayed in one place for more than a year, why she's been married to every name in Paul Simon's song "50 Ways to Leave Your Lover," and why after a summer at sleepaway camp, she sat my sister and me down to tell us we needed to go live with our father because she didn't "know how to be a mom anymore." (All of this was a step up from *her* mom, a lady who allowed my sister and me to sleep in cribs when we visited up until age nine.)

At times she felt like my child, especially when she would remind me that in another lifetime, I was the parent and she was the daughter. But mostly she felt like an older sister I was always trying to keep up with.

And according to everyone around me, I had it great! My mom was the "fun mom." She was the woman who had her nipple pierced in front of my eighth-grade boyfriend. The woman who one time disclosed to a table full of dinner guests that I had recently taken a Bic razor and accidentally given my pussy a mohawk. And the woman who, when I was fifteen, told me I needed to get a fake ID if I wanted to keep hanging out with her.

"It's just the way it is. You have one week to figure it out before your spring break," Mom threatened through the phone. At this point, I was living with my dad in Arizona, but every March I went out to visit my mom in San Diego for a week of mother/daughter debauchery.

"I'm serious, Jen. I had like three IDs when I was your age. Maybe four."

"You were dating a drug dealer! I live in Scottsdale." I tried to contain my barking so as not to let my father hear our discussion.

"Just figure it out. Okay?" I heard the click of her thirty-pound cell phone hanging up.

There was no way I was going to figure it out. I was a sophomore in high school in one of the most conservative states in the country. I was a prep who wore business suits to school and carried a briefcase. I took myself incredibly serious and always threw big words around to let my peers know I was destined for a better life than them. The downside of elitism in high school is not having access to any illegal shit. I was on student government and the president of FACS (Fine Arts Community Service, a fake club I made up strictly for college applications). I had a gay boyfriend who claimed to be straight but was still on the tumbling team, and the two of us spent our wildest nights dancing around my bedroom acting out the *Aladdin* soundtrack. I would never even have seen marijuana if it weren't for my mom having gotten me stoned the summer before eighth grade because she felt it might prevent me from smoking cigarettes.

I decided the easiest route would be to look for an older person I resembled, then ask them if they had a spare credit card, license, or gym membership with their birthday on it that I could possibly borrow. Unfortunately, everyone I approached seemed uneager to help.

So I arrived in San Diego the following week empty-handed.

"Unbelievable," my mom moaned as she handed me her coffee mug filled with Coors Light and flipped a U-turn out of the airport.

For the first two days, we lay low. We saw a few movies, tried to talk about periods, and even played a couple rounds of "Which of your husbands had the most money?" But by the end of the week, my mom was restless and in need of a bronski. She decided our only option was to cross the border into Mexico.

"Nobody cards in Mexico!" she said, slipping into a bikini.

"I still think you have to be eighteen."

"You're basically eighteen. Want a thong or a full bottom?"

she asked, holding up two equally slutty bikinis, the kind I imagine she got for free with her last six-pack of beer.

Within the hour, we were headed south. We stopped to pick up Mandy, my mom's manicurist, and Mandy's cokehead sister, Cody. Mandy was petite, redheaded, and surprisingly not Asian. She met my mom at a Shirley MacLaine "past lives" seminar in La Jolla several years prior and had been doing her acrylic French manicures ever since. She had a boyfriend I still don't believe existed and a secret tattoo of flames just above her vagina, which she constantly flashed to strangers as if it were the most hilarious thing ever. Mandy was one of those seemingly innocent, shy girls from a wealthy family who mysteriously ends up stripping in college and having eight abortions and an annulled marriage to a guy named Feather.

Her little sister was a different story. Cody looked like she'd been hanging on to the back of a motorcycle since the late '80s. She was at least six feet tall with teal hair and a bald spot near her bangs, which she used to pick and eat. She was thirty, which to me at fifteen meant her life was pretty much over. Cody was a bad drunk before she started drinking. She was brash and sloppy and always had one nipple peeking out of her lace halter top. It was hard to believe she and Mandy knew each other, let alone shared the same parents. My mom, Mandy, and Cody all had college degrees, financial stability, and the right to vote. But looking around the car, it was obvious that, even without a license, I'd be the driver getting us home.

After a thirty-five-minute ride past the border, we were in Rosarito Beach, Mexico. Rosarito is a coastal town on the Baja Peninsula notorious for fun, sun, and underage drinking. Tourism dominated the Anglo-friendly economy. You couldn't walk ten feet without accidentally getting your hair braided or having someone write your name on a grain of rice. The lobster tacos and ocean views were without comparison, but the real reason everyone congregated there was to drink their body weight in cervezas.

The girls and I pulled into Papas and Beer around twelve noon. By twelve fifteen, I was being turned away for being underage.

"But she forgot her ID in the car," my mom insisted to the bouncer.

"Then go back to your car. Isn't that it right there?" He pointed to the convertible we'd just hopped out of, no more than twenty feet from where we were currently standing.

Busted. She took a different approach.

"Fine, we'll go in. Jen, wait in the car." When the bouncer wasn't looking, she whispered in my ear for me to meet her behind the club. "I guess she's just gonna wait in the car," Mom announced, as if the thought of me not having fun was somehow going to guilt the bouncer into breaking the law.

I wandered around back and saw a large fence covered in black tarp separating the club from the rest of the beach. I tried to look in but saw nothing. Exhausted, I bought a mango on a stick, sat down by the fence, and considered getting a caricature of my head riding a whale while I waited for my mom's plan B to go into effect. I fantasized about ditching my mom and her posse and disappearing into the streets of Rosarito. Maybe my mom would think I'd been kidnapped and frantically search for me. Maybe I'd meet a new Mexican mom who made tortillas from scratch and loved doing my laundry.

This obviously wasn't the first time I'd gotten wrapped up in one of her harebrained schemes. As children, my sister and I watched her almost get arrested in the middle of the night for public nudity after the three of us were caught doing something she fondly referred to as "butt waving" on Coronado Beach. Butt waving is where you go to the beach late at night, strip off your clothes, and basically moon the waves. The result feels like a cross between a bidet and a freezing cold colonic, but as a kid, or a heavily intoxicated parent, it was thrilling. Then there was the time she broke her leg, drunkenly trying to climb the cupboards in our kitchen. She claimed she was fine, sober, and totally didn't need a doctor, suggesting instead that we pour dish soap and water all over the linoleum floor and turn the room into an indoor bubble lake. After seven minutes, she was in so much pain that my sister and I had to raft into the living room and call an ambulance. I was used to my mom being nuts, but like all kids, my willing suspension of disbelief made every time feel like the first. (Except when she misjudged and waxed off my right eyebrow before my freshman formal; that time it felt like she needed to die.)

Fishing mango hairs out of my teeth, I heard struggling on the other side of the fence, then vague whispers, followed by my mom's hands popping out and pinching my ass.

"Mom? What are you doing?" I asked her hands.

I could hear Cody's voice in reply. "We are digging you in!" she said, overly excited, confirming my suspicions that she was a total coke whore.

"Jesus!" I whispered through the fence. "You guys are a disaster. Please, just leave me out here. I'll meet up with you later."

These three weren't exactly the Viet Cong when it came to digging tunnels, but they seemed determined to make their plan work. I stood up with my back to the fence, looking around once more for my future Mexican mother, when two sets of hands gripped onto my ankles and pulled my legs out from under me. Once I was on my stomach, it was too late to fight it. Half my body was inside the club.

"Okay, Jen! Now push the rest through!" coached my mom, a regular Bela fucking Karolyi. I couldn't push. I was buried in sand, and there was nothing to grip on to. I tried to rock back and forth, but it was useless.

"I'm stuck!" I shouted loud enough that the guy selling mangos came rushing over to see if I was okay.

"¿Está todo bien?"

I looked at him hard, sending the universal look that translates to "my mom is unstable," and reached up to him for help. While at the same time, my mom and her weird friends started tugging on me from the *other* side.

"You guys, let go! I'm not coming in!" I shouted through the fence. My legs kicked and squirmed until they had at last emerged and rejoined the rest of my body on the beach.

About half an hour later, my mom and her posse came out to meet me.

"We were gonna leave immediately, but they wouldn't let us take our drinks," explained Mandy.

"Should we try a different bar?" my mom suggested.

"No! I'm done! This is stupid!" I said. I began walking away.

"Just remember, you chose me, Jen! You could have just as easily reincarnated yourself into a family with a normal mom, but how boring would that be?" she rationalized in true narcissistic form.

Before I could gain any real distance, an American couple stopped me.

"Excuse us, do you guys know where Papas and Beer is?" asked the man.

"It's—," I started, before my mom cut me off.

"You wouldn't by chance have an ID we could buy off you for my daughter, would you?" I took a second look at the woman and realized she did kind of resemble me.

Karen Bryce Masters was five feet six inches and 120

pounds, with sandy blond hair and green eyes. Everything about her matched me more or less perfectly, aside from the fact that she was fifteen years my senior. I don't remember much more about her except that she was a Leo, lived at 2454 Mango Way, Del Mar, California, 92014, and didn't plan on donating her organs.

"Umm. Well, I don't need your money, but I did just get a new license and I still have my old, almost-expired one if you want it."

"We totally aren't weirdos," Cody inserted in a creepy weirdo voice. She was dripping in post-coke-binge sweat and, after only an hour in the heat, starting to look like the Trash Heap from *Fraggle Rock*.

"I just want my daughter to be able to hang with us, you know?" said my mom, flashing her perfect, capped-tooth smile.

Karen and her boyfriend lightened up once they realized my mom was, in fact, my mom.

"Wow, you are so cool! My parents would never take me out to bars," said Karen, handing me the ID and shooting me a look that implied she too hated her mother, but for the opposite reasons.

"Kinda the coolest." My mom smirked. I could see her landing a perfect backflip in her mind.

"Thank you so much," Cody added. "We promise she won't get caught with it, or get you in any kind of trouble, or say that we ever met, or that her mom offered you money, or that you were kind of totally fine with a kid having it, knowing she was underage and probably using it to—," she nervously babbled before Karen's boyfriend mercifully cut her off.

"Just—be safe."

* * *

That day we went everywhere. And after several hours of sun and margaritas, I probably did look twenty-seven. Granted, most of the time it was hard to see my face because some guy with a whistle had me bent over a barstool, funneling tequila down my throat. Before I had Karen, I was more or less apathetic about going to bars. Growing up with alcohol being not only suggested but encouraged, I never had a deep desire for it. My only real objective was to appease my mom. But once Karen was secured under the plastic window in my wallet, she felt kind of empowering. She allowed me to sort of step away from myself. When I walked into a room as Karen, the weight of being my mother's keeper was lifted. I could detach and almost have a modicum of fun. It wasn't my problem if my mom and Cody were on top of the bar, swinging their bras around like lassos. Karen knew those strange women only peripherally, and she was far too mature to judge others.

I went home to Arizona the following week like a conquering hero. Whispers of Karen were all over school, and before lunch, I'd earned the approval of five different cliques, who all asked if I'd buy them beer. I was too scared to actually use Karen on American soil, but I did practice signing her signature at least ten times a day, just in case. The truth of the matter was that I had no real need for her. My gay boyfriend didn't want the carbs, and all my other friends were prudes. Eventually, I passed Karen off to my friend Sky, who just transferred to another school and needed an ID to hang out with her Mexican drug lord boyfriend. Even after Karen expired, Sky claimed to have used her successfully all through college.

I'm thirty-three now, and I can calmly walk into a bar through the front door. Though I have been known to tunnel out on occasion. Especially when my mom's bra is in sight.

2.

Whine Kampf

Bruno was down on one knee, holding out a ring that looked like it came from an arcade claw machine. His eyes smirked with the confidence of a soap opera bimbo who fucks only in front of a full-length mirror.

"Jen, will you be engaged to me?" he said, hitting the *g*'s in the word "engaged" with a little extra phlegm, his guttural German accent showing.

"I . . . I hate you," I said, stunned, before grabbing my purse and searching for mints. I'd just made myself throw up five pounds of garlic knots in the bathroom minutes earlier, and my mouth was still a war zone. I was trapped on the San Diego harbor cruise my mom ostensibly booked as a bon voyage dinner for Bruno. As the ship made its way back into port, I slunk down in my curiously flimsy folding chair and asked the universe three questions: Why the fuck did I just get proposed to? Where the fuck is my mother? And, how the fuck many garlic knots are still floating around in my stomach?

I met Bruno when I was in high school, where he was the creepy foreign exchange student and I was popular (among the nerds). I convinced myself he was a vampire because of his long nails, long hair, obscure accent, pencil-thin mustache, translucent skin, and uncanny ability to appear out of nowhere when I least expected. I didn't think much of him then—aside from occasionally giving him a lift off campus during lunch so long as he sat in the backseat and didn't smoke his cigarillos on me. He was obnoxious and disgusting, and he always smelled like ham. The day his exchange program ended, I assumed, would be the last time I laid eyes on him. I was wrong.

Three years later, I'd just turned twenty and was studying for the summer in Paris. Everything about France was romantic and made me long for a boyfriend who owned a Vespa and couldn't pronounce my name. I took myself very seriously and would sit in cafés for hours writing hacky Gertrude Stein–esque ramblings about how I hated my parents and held capitalism partially responsible for my anorexia.

One afternoon, sitting in a park in the sixth arrondissement, pretending to be Anaïs Nin because she seemed hotter than Gertrude Stein, I noticed a series of numbers on the back of a card in my journal. Having never been to Europe, I didn't know until getting there that these numbers were, in fact, a phone number. The card was from Bruno. He was a classical guitarist (hence the long nails), and this was a flyer for a performance he thought I'd give a shit about that happened two years before I met him.

Having nothing to lose, feeling lonely and more than a little curious, I went to a pay phone in my hotel lobby and placed the call. *It's been three years,* I thought. *People change. Who knows, maybe he has short nails now.*

The phone beeped for two long beats before a woman answered on the other end. She spoke German, and I couldn't understand a word.

"Calling for Bruno. Ob-sessed-with-me." I tried to explain, but it was no use.

We struggled back and forth for several more minutes before she said something and hung up. I placed the phone back on the receiver when instantly it started ringing. Apprehensive, I picked up.

"Hello," I said, suspicious.

"Jen. It's Bruno," a voice declared from the other side.

His accent was thick, more German than I remembered. But there was something else different about him, a confidence I hadn't noticed before. The more he spoke, the more I felt the old Bruno fade away, giving way to an erudite, worldly young man who most definitely didn't smell of ham. He asked if I had plans for the weekend and suggested we meet up in Munich. Overwhelmed by his aggressiveness, I agreed.

The nine-hour train ride to Munich was intimidating and more than a little sexy. I listened to Bjork and pictured myself in the "Jóga" music video—whenever I wasn't mentally counting my daily caloric intake. It was pitch black when the train pulled into Munich Central Station. *"Ach Ich Ich Ick Ack Euch . . . ,"* was all I heard blaring out of loudspeakers through the terminal. I translated this to mean, "Greetings, Jew-spawn with a shiksa nose."

As my anxiety mounted, I walked faster. Suddenly, a hand reached out and touched the back of my shoulder. I turned around to see a mini Joseph Fiennes circa *Shakespeare in Love* smiling at me with a bouquet of daisies in his hand. Bruno was a man now—a little man, with daintier hands than me, but still a man. His hair was cut short and his face was clean shaven save for two thin strips of muttonchops framing his cherubic jaw.

"Jallo, Jen," he said in a tone that made me forget he used to pin his bun up with chopsticks.

I smiled and followed him to his car, debating in my head whether or not I'd make out with him later that night.

By day, Munich was vast, green, and hotter than a packed boxcar. It was July, and the streets were filling with tourists. The city itself was stunning, and for me and my anorexia, the beer gardens proved infinitely scarier than any concentration camp. Bruno showed me castles and concert halls as he caught me up to speed on the last three years of his life. He told me how he was getting a master's in economics in Germany while simultaneously getting a master's in classical guitar in Yugoslavia, his parents' native country. He told me how he was trapped in Belgrade earlier that year when Clinton "drop bombs" on Milosevic to encourage his withdrawal from Kosovo.

"Nobody in Belgrade even knew what was going on in Kosovo. And yet, innocent people, women and children, lost their homes . . . their lives. . . ." He trailed off into a posttraumatic trance.

When he came to, he went on to describe how the German embassy vanished overnight and how he was forced to escape Serbia by boat to Hungary with a fake passport and a loaf of bread. Bruno considered Americans ignorant of the world outside, as he put it, "their little island."

Hypnotized by his filmworthy story, I never wanted to set foot on American soil again. I wanted to run away with Bruno and right every wrong ever inflicted upon anyone ever! This was intense shit, and there was nothing left to do but embrace it fully. Perched under a tree in a giant beer garden full of simple sugars, I leaned in and kissed Bruno on the mouth.

Later that night, I was completely smitten and past the point of making logical sense about anything. Bruno stood on the platform watching me board my train back to Paris with damp eyes and a heavy heart.

"I'm ashamed of my country and I want to be with you! Maybe forever!" I screamed out my window as he jogged alongside me. Seconds later, he jumped on the train, grabbed me again, and made out with me until we reached Stuttgart.

"When will I see you?" he screamed, waving his fanny pack.

"Soon!" I promised.

Back in Paris, I looked at all the American college boys and scoffed. I thought about how prosaic their lives were. What war did they ever find themselves stuck in? Bruno and I transcended summer-love bullshit. Together, we were going to save the world and start a revolution. My cause was still unclear, but in time I had no doubt the universe would reveal it to me. So in the meantime, I just accepted that I was a great humanitarian and lay low while I awaited further instructions.

After my studies ended, I took the first train out of Paris to Mannheim, Germany. Bruno, along with his parents, greeted me when I arrived. We went back to Bruno's house (yes, he still lived with his parents) and had cake and cigarillos. Not only was I an amateur smoker, but I'd also never smoked in front of anyone's parents in my life. It was sort of liberating how they didn't seem to give a fuck and even offered me a pipe for my tobacco, as if I were Sherlock Holmes. *So maturely European,* I thought. Neither of his parents spoke English, so the conversation was mainly just a series of head nods and giggles. At one point I drew a stick figure of my father, then exed out three different wives. Bruno's mom gasped and shook her head, thinking I was saying that my dad killed the women. Through the gift of interpretive dance, for which I have zero gift, I managed to clarify that he was just divorced but that there was one step-mom I wished he'd killed because she was a cunt. As the night drew to a close, Bruno's mother escorted me to Bruno's bedroom, which she tidied up with new sheets and bedding. She tucked us into bed and turned out the lights as she left.

Maybe this isn't totally fucking weird. Maybe in Europe all twenty-year-old men live with their parents and get tucked into bed at night by their mothers. Maybe, but I didn't care either way. I was too caught up in the idea of Bruno, the brooding musician who caused me to forsake my American ideologies and question everything I ever believed in. I wasn't going to let a little infantilizing dissuade me.

That night, with his parents mere feet away, Bruno and I made love. It was unique for several reasons:

1. He wasn't circumcised. His penis looked like a normal penis wearing a skin turtleneck.
2. He had a tramp stamp tattoo, just above his ass, of a dolphin jumping into a cluster of stars.
3. I was apparently Bruno's first.

The next day Bruno and I walked around Heidelberg with our tongues stuck eight inches down each other's throats, only breaking hold for rehydration and bathroom breaks. As dusk settled over the city, Bruno seemed to be growing more and more anxious.

Dear God, was I right about him all those years ago? Was he a vampire? Was our consummation morphing him back into the monster?

I didn't know what to do, so I just tried to keep my cool. Sweat seemed to pour down his face every time we made eye contact. We met up with some of his friends at a discotheque called Bikini that was straight out of 1989. I assessed the scene and instantly determined I was the coolest person for miles. Dudes were wearing neon gummy bracelets and high-waisted

Guess jeans and the women all had side poytails and looked like they were being roofied with human growth hormones. Partying in a sea of people who would have gotten stabbed at my high school helped me momentarily forget about Bruno's anxiety and my eating disorder. I basked in how superior I was to everyone else in the building. *I'm the hippest, skinniest girl here, and I fucking* love *my body!* I thought, dancing around like I was Kate Moss in a CK One ad. When it was time to go, Bruno tapped me on the shoulder with his baby hand and helped me down from the giant birdcage I was swinging in. We hopped in his car and prepared to leave when suddenly, he slammed the brakes and jumped out. I sat there confused as he bolted back into the club filled with Hypercolor T-shirts. Through the front entrance, I could see him talking frantically to some guy. He returned to the car with his friend Leo, a Mohawk in a fishnet tank. They mumbled back and forth in hushed tones for several minutes before addressing me directly.

"We have to go to the hospital," Bruno said.

"Wha—? Why? For who?" I was scared.

"For you," he stoically replied.

I thought, *I'm sorry, what the fuck are you talking about?*

"Meine Mutter is eine Krankenschwester komm vorbei," said Leo.

I still didn't speak German, so I didn't know what was happening. Was it time for my steroid injection? Was my boyfriend an incubus? Would I eventually look like a total cougar dating an ageless undead boy with porcelain fingers?

Leo accompanied us to a small house mere blocks away. He walked in front and greeted the woman standing in the doorway, who I eventually gleaned was his mother. More German was exchanged as she appraised me like a piece of meat. The only thing preventing me from having a panic attack was the pride I took in knowing I was *definitely* the hottest/skinniest girl Bruno had ever been seen with. Bruno explained that Leo's mom was a nurse, and they were inquiring where we could find some morning-after pills.

Apparently, Bruno was concerned he'd knocked me up. And now, apparently, everyone in his goddamned village was concerned he'd knocked me up.

When you can't speak a language, the impression you make on others is really determined by how your translator presents you. And my translator was presenting me like a fucking asshole. As soon as it dawned on me that Leo's mom wasn't checking me out because I was an adorable specimen clearly out of Bruno's league, but because she thought I was some mail order cum receptacle, I was pissed.

"But you wore a condom and didn't even cum inside me!" I explained.

"Jen, women can get pregnant with what happens first, 'before-cum,' you know?" he said condescendingly.

He insisted we go to a pharmacy the next morning for, as he put it, a "baby-killing pill."

The next day, as instructed, we went to the pharmacy and got a pill. I swallowed it and waited for Bruno's nonexistent child to die inside me. In retrospect, I probably should have extricated myself from the relationship after that. However, the drama surrounding our union was enough to hold my interest for another two and a half years.

Every three months, Bruno and I would take turns flying to see each other. After the first year and a half, I spoke fluent German, was completely anesthetized to goatees, and loved weighing myself in kilograms. I'd graduated college a year early and was content with a geographically unrealistic partnership that enabled me to avoid reality. The majority of our relationship took place over the phone, saving me tons of calories in unswallowed semen. Bruno lived on another continent, where he couldn't see the effects of my now massive eating disorder, and thought my being in a commercial meant I'd made it in Hollywood. The truth was, I was freshly out of rehab for anorexia, being supported by my father, and not even a SAG member. But Bruno helped me see how trivial my problems were in juxtaposition to those of the rest of the world. Whenever I tried to talk about being afraid of cashews, he'd say something like, "I'm afraid of flagrant Western interference disrupting the political process in the Balkans."

What I'm trying to say is, he could kind of be a dick. But at this particular time in my life, I told myself that I needed my worldview broadened by a dick, even if he did wear ascots and stonewashed denim jeans jackets. I believed in him, trusted him, and subscribed fully to his rigid ideals, including his belief that Kylie Minogue was the next John Lennon.

But for all the insights Bruno offered, he was still just twenty-two. And ours was the quintessential young love destined for a fiery plane crash into a tall building.

It was late July, Bruno and I had just spent two weeks together pretending to be an autonomous adult couple in Los Angeles, and now it was time for him to head back to his parents' basement in Deutschland. His flight departed out of San Diego, so we decided to spend our last few nights at my mom's latest condo, in the Gaslamp Quarter. She welcomed us down and was more than happy for the excuse to spend a few days living with her new boyfriend across the hall.

Craig was fifteen years her junior and closer to my age than to hers. He was a strapping Navy SEAL type who, if he didn't already have a tribal tattoo, was definitely sketching one. Craig had a naïveté that screamed "one day one of my totally hetero guy friends is going to try to suck my dick and I'm gonna be completely shocked but probably not stop him." I knew he and Bruno would have zero in common, so I kept their interaction brief in the hopes of avoiding another lecture from Bruno about the merits of socialism. My mom was constantly introducing me to new dudes who I knew I'd be lucky if I saw more than once. I found the best way to deal with this was to act really interested, talk about the future a lot, then erase them from my memory the minute they were out of arm's length.

Bruno and I spent the rest of the day shopping around town and talking obnoxiously loudly about how offended we were by SUVs. Who knows where my mom went. Much like the high school vampire, Bruno, I just assumed she morphed into a bat, a wolf, or a mist, and I'd catch up with her later.

That night, she did reappear (after sundown conveniently), and the three of us went to dinner.

"Are you two just gonna miss each other soooo much?" she asked, as if she had any concept of love.

"So much!" Bruno said. He gripped my hand like I was a child about to step in front of a bus.

"I was thinking tomorrow, for Bruno's last night, we could do the San Diego harbor cruise. Great appys, great view of the city skyline . . ." My mom trailed off, suspiciously avoiding eye contact.

"That sounds great," Bruno said.

The San Diego harbor cruise was a dinner cruise I'd gone on once when I was in eighth grade and still thought choker necklaces were cool. It was more or less a ferry that offered food, music, and a chance for people to get super wasted before fucking the same person they'd been married to for over a decade. I wasn't thrilled about the idea of spending the last night of Bruno's visit on a booze pontoon, but it did seem less macabre than making each other tear lockets, something he suggested the last time we parted.

"Okay. Cool," I conceded.

The next afternoon, my mom, Bruno, and I got dressed for the cruise. I settled on a simple sundress. Bruno went casual in his pink V-neck, pale blue jeans, and double-breasted black blazer. My mom spiced things up with a low-cut Tadashi cocktail dress and python pumps.

When we pulled into the harbor, my mom dropped off Bruno and me in front of the boat.

"You guys go grab our tickets, and I'll look for a place to park."

"You're in heels, why don't I park the car?" I said.

"I'm fine, just get our tix and I'll meet you guys in a second."

"You want me to come with you?"

"Jen. Come," Bruno said, like I was a Labrador.

We got out of the car and headed up to the ticket line. I kept a lookout for my mom while Bruno retrieved our passes.

"I don't see her," I said, scanning the lot, concerned.

"Oh, well. Let's board."

"No. Where is she? This is so weird."

"Das macht nichts. Wir gehen uns," he said sternly as he pushed me toward the dock.

I started to panic. In my youth, my mom was notorious for dropping me off someplace, saying she'd be right back, and then disappearing for days. Once, I was left for three weeks with two live-in babysitters who only cooked beans. Another time, she took me to meet a woman she worked with, asked me to go play in her backyard, and then vanished for a weekend without further explanation. When she returned, she'd always act like it was no big deal and try to distract me with some sort of embroidered airport souvenir sarong from wherever she'd just been. I got back at her later in life by sleeping with one of my stepbrothers.

"I just don't understand where she could have gone," I said, unable to focus.

I stood on the deck of the boat, looking wide-eyed and pathetic, like Fievel from *An American Tail.*

Bruno ignored me as we boarded the boat and entered the main salon. Tables separated the long windows from a simple parquet dance floor in the center of the room. The tasteful white tablecloths struggled to stay classy in a sea of folding chairs and cheap balloons. If it weren't for the crowd of retirees, I would have assumed I was crashing someone's fraternity date dash.

A waiter handed us glasses of champagne and escorted us to a small table for two perched on a tiny platform at the front of the room. Once I got to the table, I realized I'd been set up. A bottle of champagne sat waiting for us with a note. I knew it was from my mom before I even opened it.

Have a magical evening, you two! Love, The Mothership, it read.

I hated how cavalier she could be. No apology for triggering my abandonment issues, no information stating whether or not I'd ever be seeing her again. Just a "Have fun!" I wanted to have a note delivered back to her, saying, "Thanks for ruining my life."

Bruno's patience with me seemed to be dwindling, and since it was our last night together, I tried to put my anger aside.

"Prost!" he said, raising his engraved keepsake champagne flute and staring into my eyes like he was stealing my soul.

The cruise set sail just as the DJ started pumping Bonnie

Raitt's "Something to Talk About." Bruno asked me to dance and I obliged. His moves were always a bit eccentric—he loved spinning me, walking a couple feet away, then pulling me by my hair back into a dip. But there was something about him that night that seemed especially intense.

Bruno looked stoical as he sipped his champagne with his pinkie in the air and started talking about the coming months we'd be spending apart. He had to go to Yugoslavia to finish his master's then return to Germany to begin his M.B.A. Like a true German, his plan was laid out precisely. It would take no less than five years before he could even consider living in the States. And my B.A. in theater made less sense internationally than Craig's forthcoming tribal tattoo.

Dinner interrupted our conversation and helped lighten the mood. Etta James's "At Last" played softly in the background as I accidentally inhaled a whole basket of garlic knots—because I was still mad at my mom, and food represented the love she wasn't giving me.

"I love this song. I want it to play at my wedding someday," I said through a mouthful of dough.

Bruno smirked a weird "I'm Euro" smirk but said nothing.

Once I'd ingested every carb on the table, I excused myself to the bathroom. I made sure I was alone, then proceeded to use my entire fist to plunge up the five pounds of flour currently sitting in my stomach. After my recent stint in rehab, I had successfully convinced Bruno and everyone around me that I'd beaten anorexia. The truth was, rehab made me *the best anorexic ever*. Half the hospital was skinnier than me (annoying), so I had to learn new tricks in order to keep up. One of those tricks was bulimia. According to my then roommate, who'd recently been put on a feeding tube and looked great, you could eat whatever you wanted as long as you threw it all back up within thirty minutes of swallowing. Any longer would result in absorption of sugars, fats, and feelings.

Working yourself into vomiting feels kind of like working yourself into orgasm. You basically rub back and forth along the back of your throat until you explode. Once you are finished, you're left with a nose full of snot, the worst breath in the world, and an overall sense of euphoria. Eventually my behavior led to the loss of my period, most of my hair, and my entire social circle (made up of two people). But like all addictions, when you are in them, they seem like the best idea in the world.

I quickly washed my hands up to my elbows, blew my nose, wiped the tears from my eyes, and walked back to the table. When I returned, a chocolate lava cake covered in a mountain of whipped cream was waiting. Suspecting nothing, I watched as Bruno stood up to pull out my chair.

"Ich liebe dich so sehr mein schatz," Bruno professed.

"Ich dich auch," I replied, locking eyes with the lava cake.

Just then, Etta James's "At Last" kicked in again, only this time louder.

I looked over to the DJ, who seemed to be staring directly at me. As the music continued, Bruno took a deep breath, rolled out of his chair, and crawled over to me on his knees.

"Wha—? What are you doing?" I was scared to hear his answer.

"Jen, will you be engaged to me?" He opened up a small box that must have been hiding in his ass. Inside the box was a small white gold band with a tiny sapphire embedded between two diamond chips. Now, look, I didn't want to get engaged regardless of what kind of ring Bruno had. But, come on, diamond chips? This felt like some kind of cheap move my dad would pull. The only other time I'd seen diamonds that small was when my father bought me studs for my eighth birthday instead of the dog I'd been begging for. A week into wearing them, the diamonds slipped backwards through my ear holes and were gone forever.

"Well?" asked Bruno, looking back for support from the sea of strangers awaiting my response.

"I . . . I hate you," I said.

Before I elaborated, Bruno interpreted my "I hate you" to be less of an "I don't want to do this" and more of an "Oh shucks, you got me," and forced the ring down my swollen, bulimic finger.

The crowd erupted in applause.

"No, wait, I can't do this," I whispered.

Bruno looked at me in utter disbelief, his hand still covered in the whipped cream he no doubt planned to plant on my nose, then lick off with a kiss. He got up from his knee and sat down quietly as the cruise pulled back into port.

As we disembarked, we were bombarded by pats on the back and congratulatory high fives. Bruno refused to look at me. We walked silently to the nearest cab and jumped in. Neither of us spoke a word until we were back at my mom's apartment.

When I opened the door, my mom and her meathead boyfriend were waiting for us.

"Show us the ring, you engaged gal!" she said.

This was irritating on two levels: one, the fact that my mom aided in Bruno's ambush; and two, the fact that my mom didn't have any problem with her barely-out-of-college, anorexic, underemployed daughter getting engaged to a kid who lived on the other side of the world.

"Mom, can I speak to you alone for a minute?" I said.

Once we were in her bedroom with the door securely shut, I lost it. *"What were you thinking, letting that happen!"*

"What do you mean? You aren't happy? But you love Bruno."

"I'm twenty-two years old. I don't know what I love!"

"So you don't want to move to the next level with your relationship? You guys have been together for two whole years."

"Mom, I know that sounds like a long time to you, but imagine if you'd married the guy you were dating at twenty-two."

"I did," she said.

"Exactly!"

Eventually she apologized and promised to be on my team for the remainder of Bruno's stay (about eight more hours).

Knowing Bruno and I had some talking to do, mom and her dildo with a face retreated to his apartment across the hall. Bruno was busy throwing around all his low-cut V-necks when I finally asked if we could talk.

"*Es gibt nichts zu sagen,* Jenny," he said, unwilling to talk.

"I'm really sorry. I just think we are both too young to be doing something like getting married."

"Who's talking about being married? This is about being engaged. Promising ourselves to each other for all of eternity, like our tear lockets."

"Maybe what you really mean is you want me to wear a promise ring?"

"What's that?"

"Well," I said, "it signifies that we're in an exclusive relationship but not making any rash decisions about the future. I'll totally wear it if we can agree that's what it symbolizes." In the right light, the ring did kind of look cute on me.

"No!" he said, snatching the ring off my hand. "I don't know what I'm going to do with these. I can't return them."

"Them?"

Bruno reached into his purple nylon duffel bag and produced a matching ring. "I got myself one too."

Things were getting worse by the minute. Bruno not only wanted to be engaged, but he also wanted to wear matching engagement rings, and to top it all off, his finger was thinner than mine!

Bruno picked up the phone and called himself a cab while I thought about how to diet my finger down to a more competitive size. He glared at me as he rattled off my mother's address and asked that the car come as soon as possible. I followed Bruno down to the lobby, trying desperately to assuage his animosity.

"I don't want you to leave on bad terms," I said, noticing a cab painted like a mini Shamu wearing a birthday hat pull up behind us.

"Jen, it's too late." He was somber. The smiling Shamu face seemed to mock him behind his back.

"You're not going to kill yourself, are you?" I asked, half worried and half curious.

Bruno didn't answer, but he did hand me back the engagement ring.

"Keep it, throw it in a drawer, it doesn't matter," he said, defeated, before locking himself inside Shamu's belly and driving away.

I didn't speak to Bruno for several weeks after that and was completely devastated in the way all twenty-two-year-olds are when their first long-distance lover tries to pirate their future. When we did speak, things seemed different. It was as if we'd peeked into the future and realized that for us, as a couple, there wasn't one. Our fear of change kept us on the phone and in denial for a good three months more before I finally lashed out and fucked my forty-year-old circumcized neighbor.

As time went on, Bruno and I eventually lost touch completely. From time to time, I do think of him. I hope that he's able to look back on our time together with fondness. I really do wish the best for him. But he isn't on Facebook, Twitter, JDate, or any other social media site I've searched, so it's safe to assume he killed himself.

3.

All the Best Men Are Either Gay, Married, or Your Therapist

There are two types of people in the world: those who think everyone needs therapy, and those who have never been. My parents divorced when I was an infant. I've been dyslexic, anorexic, and a theater major, so it's fairly obvious which category I fall under.

Throughout my childhood, my parents dropped me off at a multitude of therapists' offices in hopes that I'd avoid growing up to be the kind of asshole who writes books about them. Also because it was sometimes easier than finding a nanny. And as a result, I'm one of those therapy junkies that believes I'd be a fraction of the person I am if I didn't have fifty to ninety minutes a week of somebody's undivided attention.

I was six years old when I was shown my first Rorschach test. (I think I saw a Boston terrier driving a Camaro.) Dr. Rob, my child psychologist at the time, used to watch me play with shapes and clay while subtly trying to decipher whether or not I'd grow up to be a raging psychopath. He'd ask me questions like, "If you were leaving town on a boat and there were only three seats, whom would you take with you?" I remember his alarm when I gave my toy poodle, Bouncer, all three seats, after prefacing that my little sister would start a mutiny if granted permission to board. At that time, it was obvious to even my poodle that my sister most likely had a personality disorder and that I would make an impressively level-headed captain of an imaginary boat.

When I was sixteen and having panic attacks, I saw Bethany Fryman, an M.F.T. who lived on my street. Bethany was a morbidly obese grandma who studied Carl Jung and smelled like a Cinnamon Roll Yankee Candle. She blamed my mom for everything, which I assume had something to do with the fact that she was being paid by my father. Bethany came to all my high school plays and even wrote me a letter of recommendation for college. I think she's dead now.

At twenty, I developed an eating disorder and started seeing Pamela Mann, a nutritional therapist I met at LA Fitness. Pamela was fifty but looked thirty. She loved jewelry and would always talk about redesigning her late mother-in-law's brooches. We had dinner a few times, and I think once I even went on a date with her son (small penis).

I terminated with Mona, the lesbian L.C.S.W. from Calabasas, after she tried to hypnotize me and steal my car at my twenty-eighth birthday party.

Unable to find the kind of treatment I needed (that is, someone who wouldn't steal my car), I went to graduate school to get my own degree in the field. Like a pot dealer who sells only to smoke for free, a master's in psychology seemed like a great way to help people while helping myself in the process. I was also out of work as an actress and needed something to say when people asked the dreaded question, "Soooo, what are you working on?"

Graduate school was composed of twenty-something degree collectors who didn't want to face the real world, older women whose kids were out of the house and whose husbands were sick of looking at them, and lost souls whose plan A wasn't covering their rent. I was positive my involvement was a complete anomaly.

"You know, just something to do in between gigs," I explained to the guy who handed me a ticket to park in the school lot.

I walked into my first class with the kind of "I want to see how your side lives, but I'm still sort of looking down on you" swagger I picture Colin Farrell having when he does a ride-along with the NYPD to get in character for a role. I avoided sitting next to any angry cat ladies and instead plopped down next to a nonthreatening gay guy.

Eric was in his mid-thirties with blond scruffy hair, designer jeans, and several sandalwood bracelets that let me know he had his life together. I was confiding in him that I wasn't sure what I'd gotten myself into and that I'd probably be getting a super-important acting gig that would force me to cut my studies short, but that it was nice getting to know him regardless—when the teacher, a spitting image of Wallace Shawn who I'm still not entirely convinced wasn't Wallace Shawn, walked in.

"Yeah, everything about this place reminds me of this episode of *Strong Medicine* I once did where I—"

Professor Shawn looked at me hard and cleared his throat to shut me up. He drew a large circle in red marker on the whiteboard that I guess was supposed to symbolize how we are all one. Inside the circle, he wrote a fact he found interesting about himself. I don't remember what it was, but it's safe to assume it was something like "I eat food." He then proceeded to go around the room and ask each person to stand up and share a fact of their own. Rolling my eyes, I gave my new friend, whom I'd probably never see again because of my imminent rise to superstardom, a nudge. Eric looked back at me like he felt sorry for my lack of maturity and stood up to share.

"Well, you may not know it from looking at me . . . clean-cut prepster that I am . . . but, the reality is . . . I just got out of prison and you are the first people I've said that out loud to." Eric burst into tears, then gave the room a giant Namaste salute.

I put my hands nervously over my mouth to stop my body from doing anything stupid, like laughing uncontrollably or choking, and tried to remain open-minded about the slight detour my life had taken.

As a master's student, it's mandatory that you go to therapy for at least two semesters. The fee is waived and the school gives you a list of preapproved professionals to choose from. I perused the names carefully to make sure I didn't see the Calabasas car thief and eventually settled on Dr. Carl Sandford. I thought it might be interesting to try working with a man for a change, and since I wasn't paying for it, and people like Eric were allowed to hold master's degrees, I figured I'd go with a more expensive, less prisoner-y Ph.D.

After a quick chat over the phone, Dr. Carl gave me a time to come see him in his Beverly Hills office. Around 3 P.M. the next day, I pulled into an underground parking garage in work-out gear most real workout people would classify as "pajamas" and rushed inside to "sort of" make my 2:45 appointment time.

I walked into a tastefully decorated waiting room and sat down. The coffee table in front of me was scattered with various magazines, which I took to be my first test. And though I was tempted to check out Angelina Jolie as shot by Brad Pitt for *W* magazine, my ego and need for approval made me choose *The Economist.* I know I didn't know him, had never seen him in my entire life, and might never see him again because I was about get famous, but like any first date, I wanted Dr. Carl to think I was smart and better than the real me actually was. Within minutes, the adjacent door leading to his office flung open and a dapper man in his late forties was revealed.

Dr. Carl wore a dark velvet blazer with a white button-down shirt underneath, no tie, great shoes, and casual pants. He was handsome in a daddy-figure way and seemed to possess a flair for the dramatic. Tussling his almost inappropriately long hair out of his face, he motioned for me to follow him down the hall into his corner office. He walked with purpose, and I almost scored a second workout just trying to keep up with him.

Inside his office, everything was made of dark wood. He owned one of those giant wingback chairs, which instantly made me kind of pissed that all psychologists didn't have them. Note to all therapists everywhere: Wingback chairs legitimize you!

Dr. Carl curled up into his seat Indian-style as he started asking questions. "So, why are we here?"

"I'm a student at Antioch and—"

He cut me off. "Why are we *really* here?"

"Well, we are here because I'm here and you're here. . . ." I waited for his eyes to give me some kind of hint that I was on the right track.

Dr. Carl continued to stare straight through me, which in turn forced me to ramble. I pulled out all the buzzwords I could think of.

"I've been in and out of treatment since I was six years old. I'm somewhat of a perennial child with abandonment issues and a serious attachment disorder. My mother is a narcissistic love junkie and my father is a controlling egomaniac, so obviously I was never *seen,* and as a result became a fucking actor. I'm not really into drugs or alcohol, but I do get a high off starving myself. I've been on Zoloft for the last four years. I'd be up for a little cog behavioral work here and there. I'd even be down to explore an Electra complex if you felt I needed to. But for the most part, I'm just looking for school credit. Have you ever read *The Drama of the Gifted Child*? Mind-blowing stuff, am I right?"

Carl looked at me like I was out of my goddamn mind. "I think we should see each other twice a week."

I started seeing Dr. Carl every Tuesday and Thursday. And unlike other people I'd worked with, he tried to avoid talking about the past. He wanted to focus on the present. When Dr. Carl would get worked up, he'd always do something extra-dramatic for effect. He never did a perfect round-off back handspring across the room the way I'd hoped, but he did once crush a Starbucks cup with his forehead. He was quirky and unconventional and more or less a complete enigma.

And I loved him. Well, I guess I didn't really love him, but I thought I did, which is what good "transference" is all about. The reality was, I didn't know one thing about him. That's actually what I loved about him. That, coupled with the fact that the only thing we did when we were together was talk about me. Dr. Carl was selfless in our sessions. It was something I hadn't experienced often in life, and it made me certain he was hiding something.

Sometimes on my way out of the parking garage, I'd try to guess which car was his. I wondered if he had children, what my life would be like if he were my dad, and how big his penis was. Over time I found myself increasingly frustrated with the fact that Dr. Carl refused to disclose even the tiniest morsel about his life. I didn't feel like I was asking for too much. I just wanted to know simple things like, was he married, or totally head over heels in love with me? Anytime I tried to inquire about his personal life, he managed to avoid the question.

"Jenny, Freud would classify this line of questioning as avoidance. My relationship status is irrelevant. Nondisclosure is my policy. If I start making our time about me, that's behaving like your parents and it's retraumatizing. It can contaminate the transference, blur our boundaries, and shift your focus from yourself. Believe me, the more you know about me, the less help I'll be to you."

"Why doesn't Dr. Carl want to be friends?" I thought as I walked through the parking lot later, peering into the driver's-side window of the Mercedes E class I'd convinced myself was his.

"He's just being a tad too professional, don't you think?" I lamented to Eric one day over lunch. "Should I start wearing makeup to our sessions?"

"He's your therapist, you aren't supposed to know anything about him." Eric flossed his too-white veneers into my tuna salad.

Eric and I had become close friends. At first we were friends in the way that you are nice to your drug dealer because you don't want him to kill you, but after several weeks surrounded by menopausal women wearing their pets' ashes in lockets around their necks, we'd actually forged a bond.

"But don't you feel like he should be a little more relaxed, since my seeing him is kind of a school thing?" I Googled the words "Dr. Sandford Ph.D." on the laptop in front of me.

"Jenny, when I was in prison—" Eric started.

"Yeah, Eric! You were in prison! Shouldn't you know people who can find this shit out for me?"

"Actually, I was about to say that I reached a point of Zen, of not having to know or be in control of everything around me."

"What do you mean? Like, when you didn't have money or cigs to bargain with?"

"I *mean,* I became a better person. And so should you."

"Umm, helloo, I am in therapy, aren't I?" I said as I doodled *Mrs. Jenny Sandford* and *Dr. and Mrs. Carl Sandford* in the Moleskine notebook I'd bought from the campus bookstore.

Back in class, my fellow students shared detailed diagrams of their family systems in something we in the mental health biz referred to as a genogram. A genogram is like a family tree that also tells you how fucked up you are. It allows you to see patterns and understand family dynamics by describing each member's personality traits, medical history, and emotional relationships. It also lists any significant sideline characters such as stepchildren, therapists, and slaves. For example, a family tree might tell you I had a great-uncle on my mother's side, but a genogram would let you know that he was a homosexual alcoholic with schizophrenia and an unhealthy addiction to pretzels. I contemplated bringing my genogram home with me for Thanksgiving but worried it might turn out like the New Year's I picked everyone's resolutions out for them.

Luckily, I was interrupted by a vibration from my phone, which I was certain was the big break that would change the course of my life forever. I excused myself from the classroom and started mentally packing a sensible suitcase for next year's Sundance film festival. Outside, I opened my e-mail in-box to find a message from Dr. Carl. But it wasn't sent from the e-mail address I'd written to. This was his private e-mail!

All it said was "Yes." Just, "Yes." In retrospect, I think Dr. Carl was probably just saying yes to my request to change our appointment time the next day, but in the moment, it sure seemed like he was saying yes to every wild, warped, neurotic thought or hope I'd ever experienced under his care.

I printed out the e-mail, laminated it between two pieces of wax paper with an iron, and pasted it to my rented refrigerator.

I imagined all the questions it could be the answer to.

"Am I your favorite patient?" Yes.

"Am I your prettiest patient?" Yes.

"Don't you think I should be famous already?" Yes.

"Do you love me?" Yes.

"Is it okay that I masturbate to you sometimes?" Yes.

"Do you masturbate to me sometimes?" Yes.

"Don't you want to blur the boundaries of our relationship as much as I do?" Yes.

"Should I dye my hair red?" Yes.

"Should I dye my hair black?" Yes.

"Should I taunt people who were mean to me in high school during my future Oscars speech?" Yes.

"Should I just go ahead and put that shoe-shaped couch on a credit card because I deserve it?" Yes.

"Am I a good person?" Yes.

"Am I a *great* person?" Yes.

"Don't you wish I were your daughter?" *Yes! Yes! Yes!*

Before I got into my evening homework assignment (an essay on cultural sensitivity), I hopped on Facebook to touch base with my business contacts, letting them know I wasn't currently committed to any particular project and that if they moved quickly, they could swoop in and nab me at a reasonable rate. After writing a small essay as my status update,

I noticed new names on the right side of my screen in the "People You May Know" section.

At the top of the list was Dr. Carl.

I called Eric.

"I've been staring at it for the last half hour. It's his real page!" I shrieked as I paced around my unfurnished living room. I totally planned on buying a couch in the shape of a shoe and other trendy home furnishings just as soon as I got the next residual check from my groundbreaking guest spot on *18 Wheels of Justice,* starring Lucky Vanous on TNN.

"What can you see?"

I couldn't see much. The picture was blurry and totally not a good representation of his overall vibe. His age wasn't listed, but his birthday, February 3, was.

"I knew he was an Aquarius!" I said to Eric, whom I'd managed to lure over to my house with the promise of cupcakes I didn't actually have.

"His personal e-mail is obviously the one he uses for this stuff. That's why you couldn't find him before. Now Facebook thinks you guys are friends because he's in your e-mail contacts. Where are the cupcakes?" he asked suspiciously.

Ignoring him, I proceeded to spin out in my head.

"His bio sounds like he's Tony Robbins," I said. This was a side of Dr. Carl I really didn't know, a side that sounds more like the self-promoting, image-obsessed father I was in therapy to disentangle myself from.

"The whole reason I wanted Dr. Carl to be my dad-husband was because he was different from my current dad-husband! I mean, yes, I love that he's an Aquarius, but how am I supposed to live with the fact that he calls himself a 'therapist to the stars'? That's obviously not going to work for me as I continue to get more and more visibility. And what about the fact that he has only fifty friends? That kind of makes him seem like a loser, right?" I spun around three times as fast as I could in my swivel chair trying to un-see what I'd just seen.

Eric was half-listening, his torso now wedged into my oven, looking for cupcakes.

"Did you look at his friends?" Eric shouted, still not giving up the hunt.

I clicked to see the fifty people Dr. Carl deemed worthy of Facebook friendship. Most were randoms over forty who looked like they owned a turtleneck in every color, talked about wines like they were talking about people, and had crazy hairy vaginas.

"You don't have any cupcakes, do you?" Eric walked out of the kitchen, realizing he'd been duped.

"We can go buy some." My eyes were once again glued to the screen.

He sat down next to me and pushed my hands away from the keyboard.

"You are really bad at this." Eric zipped through Dr. Carl's friend list and clicked on a young girl with the same last name.

"How did you know—?" I started, but stopped myself just in case Eric's answer was "in prison."

"This must be his daughter." He scrolled through the girl's page.

Lisa Sandford was twenty-one, in art school, living in Santa Monica, hotter than expected, and *totally Dr. Carl's daughter.*

If Dr. Carl had a real daughter, then what did he need me for? My abandonment complex kicked into high gear. It was as if I thought I'd booked a series regular role as "Therapist's Daughter," and it turned out to be a one-day co-star as "Crazy Patient #342."

What the fuck! Not only did Dr. Carl have a child, but he had a child younger than me? I always thought he looked at me like a daughter, but now I knew he probably looked at me like someone who could babysit his daughter and probably chaperone her on a school trip to Washington, D.C.—where I'd have to use credit cards and IDs for rental cars and hotel incidentals. . . .

I was starting to panic.

Lisa had three photo albums available for perusal. I arbitrarily clicked one open and started snooping. The first album was composed mainly of her girlfriends graduating from what looked like high school. The second album seemed to depict her as someone who'd recently read *The Secret,* with lots of vision boards and comments like "Go straight."

But the third album was the jackpot. It was titled "Sandals Jamaica Christmas" and was filled with pictures of Dr. Carl, Lisa, and one of her girlfriends. One photo showed them snorkling and giving the thumbs-up. Another showed them eating conch fritters.

This album told me several things about Dr. Carl:

1. He was not with Lisa's mom,
2. He knew how to swim, and
3. Much like Professor Wallace Shawn, he ate food.

But it also got at something deeper, something almost imperceptible to the human eye: Dr. Carl was lonely. In all the pictures, his eyes just seemed to drift toward the horizon like he was in search of something he had yet to find. True love, perhaps? He was also a Beverly Hills Ph.D. who was choosing to vacation at a Sandals resort. He was better than that, but maybe he didn't think so. Maybe he came from humble beginnings, had a fear of trusting, and just never felt good enough. I was certain some if not all of this contributed to his split from Lisa's mother.

Poor Dr. Carl, I thought as I wondered what the Jamaica trip would have been like if I had been Lisa's friend. I'm sure we would have played it cool the first few days, kept our mutual attraction under wraps. Maybe we would have gone out to see a steel drum band after his daughter passed out from the muscle relaxer I put in her rum and Coke. Maybe he'd touch my leg in the cab back to the hotel. Then maybe carnal desire would win out and I'd move my toothbrush into his suite.

Eric binged on a box full of stale Cap'n Crunch left by the previous tenants and then went home. I thought about my session with Dr. Carl the next morning and wondered what, if anything, would be different now that I knew what I knew.

"Yeah, it's weird," I said, in some of my worst acting to date. "I think I'm just in need of a big vacation. Jamaica or somewhere tropical. Need to reconnect with the earth, get wet, blow some bubbles, you know?"

Dr. Carl's face gave away nothing.

"So how was your weekend? Did you get out of the house much?"

Again nothing, which I'd learned from school meant he was taking a "Rogerian stance." Basically just shutting the fuck up and waiting for me to solve my own problems. Knowing what he was up to, I continued.

"It's just kind of disconcerting that you know so much about me and yet I don't know anything about you besides that you're an Aquarius."

"And how do you know that?"

Thinking fast, I rolled my eyes and tried to cover. "Oh, come on, Doc, it's so obvious that you're an Aquarius. Like I don't know an Aquarius when I see one." I laughed nervously before plunging into a rant about how offended I was that I'd never been molested.

"I'm telling you, he's an impenetrable forest!" I told Eric over coffee. Dr. Carl's unwillingness to be straight with me was making me insane. It consumed my thoughts—and also distracted me from the fact that I was now basically living with Eric.

"I think this is just you not being able to respect boundaries or stomach rejection," he said, like he'd actually been paying attention in class.

"Obviously!" I spooned the foam off Eric's latte and ate it. "It just feels weird. He's making me feel like a total stalker."

"Well, you are. And that's okay," Eric said. *Finally,* some validation.

"You know what? I'm over it. His life is his life. Right? I can respect this bizarre nondisclosure tic of his. Besides, I'm probably seconds away from leaving grad school anyway. And don't worry, I've already told my agents I'm gonna need your airfare negotiated into any and all future contracts."

I downed the remainder of Eric's drink and motioned for the check, but before we got up, Eric grabbed my laptop.

"Just to protect you from yourself, we are going to block both Dr. Carl and Lisa, okay?" he said, logging into my Facebook.

"Fine."

"Password."

Guilt washed over my face. I bit my lip, trying to maintain calm.

"What is it? Why are you blushing?"

"No, nothing. I mean, Eric, you were in prison. Giving you any of my passwords does seem a little—"

"Bullshit," Eric said. "Dish now."

"It's *H-O-T . . . ,*" I started.

"Yeah . . ."

"*C-A-R-L.*" I exhaled.

"Hot Carl? Do you even know what that is?"

"No. What?"

"It's like when someone shits on your face," Eric said. "You've never heard of a Hot Carl? Cleveland Steamer? None of this rings a bell?"

"Eric, I'm straight."

"Wow." He lifted his eyebrows in disbelief and logged in to my page.

Then, as if he'd seen a ghost, Eric's face went white.

"What is it? Did someone I went to high school with have a stillborn or something?" I turned the laptop toward me.

The glare of the screen seemed to wash out everything but a single word:

CONGRATULATIONS!

Less than three minutes ago, Dr. Carl's daughter, Lisa, posted a picture of Dr. Carl with his new fiancée. Dr. Carl was engaged.

"She's so much older than me!" I gasped.

"Good for him," Eric replied.

"No, totally." I said, "I'm sure a woman like this will absolutely make Dr. Carl happy." I clicked on her name and went directly to her Facebook page.

Anya Finkelstrum was a forty-five-year-old wedding planner from Boston. She currently resided in Topanga Canyon, six miles away from her eighteen-year-old son, Bengie, who just started his first year of college at Pepperdine. What Anya's page didn't reveal about her, I was more than happy to make up in my head:

Anya grew up in Allentown, Pennsylvania, where her first husband, Cletus, routinely beat her. After tricking him into thinking she'd killed herself by jumping into a quarry, she changed her identity and fled to Boston with her son, à la Julia Roberts in *Sleeping with the Enemy,* until she could save enough money to move out to Encino (where a weird aunt lived) to start a new life. Convinced she'd never love again, but still a romantic at heart, Anya waited for Bengie to be old enough before going back to work full-time, this time doing something she loved: wedding planning. Anya refused to date all through Bengie's adolescence and only met Dr. Carl by accident when she got dragged to a turtleneck wine party at a close friend's house. They hit it off instantly and started what would become a full-blown courtship. Trying to show the utmost respect for Bengie and his mother's relationship, Dr. Carl didn't start sleeping over until Bengie was out of the house and away at school. Now the cat's out of the bag, Lisa's dad is fucking Bengie's mom, and everybody including Lisa can't wait to have a hand in the wedding.

No wonder he'd chosen her over me. My life story, however twisted, couldn't compete with the one I'd invented for Anya. I suddenly wished I'd made my stories in therapy more compelling. I could have worked as a child prostitute for several months on the streets of Green Bay, Wisconsin, after running away from home. I could have been a sister-wife living on a Mormon compound in Salt Lake City. I could have backpacked across Asia and been wrongly imprisoned for drug smuggling like Claire Danes in *Brokedown Palace*. I'd made the hideous mistake of being myself in therapy, and now I was just another almost-famous starlet whom he'd eventually ask to endorse his forthcoming vitamin line.

Dr. Carl was getting married—and it was none of my business.

I couldn't tell what was making me more upset: the fact that I wasn't in the know about the wedding or the fact that I wasn't *in* the wedding. Regardless of how I felt, Anya and Dr. Carl were to become one, and I had to learn to live with it.

"As, like, an exercise, I think it might be good for me to meet Anya," I whispered to Eric one day in class.

Dr. Wallace Shawn was blabbering on about how the human ego is a slave that must serve two masters: the id, the childlike pleasure-seeking part of the psyche; and the superego, its moralistic rule-dork counterpart.

"You are like a full-time id," Eric whispered back.

"I need to know who my therapist is choosing to spend the rest of his life with," I whined defensively. "Not knowing could be incredibly detrimental to my treatment. She could be a complete fucking whack job, and do I want to take love and relationship advice from a guy who's about to marry a complete fucking whack job? I don't think so."

Dr. Shawn stopped talking and glared at me with hate. Eric and I were handed our take-home midterms and asked to leave class early.

"How is it that I'm a grown adult and still getting in trouble for talking in class?" I mused.

"Because you are still doing all the same shit you probably did in high school."

"Fine, you know what? I'll go to Anya's work without you," I fumed, and walked off.

"Who said anything about going to her work?" Eric called out after me.

"Where else am I supposed to run into her?" I said, my back still turned.

"You're fucking nuts!" Eric shouted.

Maybe I was nuts, but it's not like I was going to Anya's work to threaten her life or tell her not to marry Dr. Carl. The only reason I called and made an appointment with her using a fake name was because Dr. Carl had built her up in my mind by refusing to talk about her with me. I had to meet her if I was ever going to put to rest the mystery of Dr. Carl's private life and get my treatment back on track. I gave myself a pat on the back for taking such a proactive approach to my own mental health.

When I got to Anya's office that afternoon, I paced back and forth outside, weighing what I was about to do for a good thirty seconds. Then the front door swung open.

It was Eric.

"Sweetie!" he said in a weird, low voice that he clearly thought made him sound heterosexual. "I told Ms. Finklestrum that when you scheduled, you didn't know I'd be able to take off work for this. But, well, here I am!" Eric finished with a flourish before going in for what was by far the most awkward kiss of my life.

"Sweetie. Wow. I— Just— Wow." I turned to meet Anya—*the* Anya—in person.

"Hi. I'm Anya," she said, extending the hand I had no real interest in (the right one).

"Wow, beautiful engagement ring," I said, staring at a modest two-carat cushion cut on her left ring finger.

"Thank you."

"We were thinking of just getting tattoos," Eric blurted

out. He did some sort of gay-guy hand gesture to emphasize his point.

"So what kind of wedding are you two thinking about having?" Anya asked, showing us to a nearby love seat.

"I'm not really sure yet," I said, and then slyly added: "What are you doing for *your* wedding?"

"I was thinking," Eric cut in, "of topiaries comprising succulents as centerpieces." He proceeded to out himself about five more times. "I'm into leathers and feathers, like maybe a bit of a 'Coachella, vampire, summer harvest as shot by Sofia Coppola' vibe. . . ."

Before I could do damage control, my phone vibrated with a missed call. Looking down, I saw that it was, finally, my agent. I anxiously excused myself to the restroom and was listening to the message (and possibly taking a peek in Anya's medicine cabinet) when I heard the front door open outside. I looked out and saw that, walking straight in, carrying nearly five pounds of Jerry's Famous Deli turkey sandwiches, was Dr. Carl. I closed myself back into Anya's restroom as fast as I could.

Now I know why he can never do lunch sessions, I thought to myself, enraged that I'd been passed over in favor of nosh with the fiancée.

I needed to formulate a plan. I scanned the room for a window or crawl space I could fit through.

Outside, I heard Anya introduce her fiancé to my "fiancé." This was so bad. Pacing in a small circle, I could think of nothing else to do but check my voice mail and hope my agents were outside the building, waiting to move in and extract me.

"Hey, Jenny, it's Rico. I don't know if you got my e-mail but I think it's time we let you go. Call me if you have any questions."

I took a minute to sum up the situation: I was currently locked in a bathroom, hiding from my therapist, pretending to be marrying a gay ex-con, and getting dropped by my mid-level talent agency. All at the same time.

"You okay in there, sweetie?" Eric called out meekly.

I opened the door and yanked Eric in.

"What the fucking fuck are we doing?" he screeched. "I should have never come here. This was the worst idea ever. Like, I can't even believe my life has devolved in this way. I'm even wearing agate stones to protect me against negativity, but somehow your insanity is overpowering them." He touched one of his Chan Luu wrap bracelets and backed away from me like I was that little girl from *The Ring*.

"You two okay?" Anya asked, tapping on the door.

Eric opened it slightly, making eye contact with Anya.

"We are kind of going through something and *I think we need a little space*!" he shrieked flamingly.

"Do you two want to come back at a different time? I completely understand how this stuff works and—"

"No. I think we need *you* to leave," Eric said. He sounded like a bitchy queen at the start of an ecstasy-fueled rave-rumble.

"What?" she asked, completely thrown.

"I said, my fiancée and I need a few minutes alone, and we would like you to *clear the fuck out*."

"Um. Okay. Sure. We'll just take a walk around the block," Anya said, cowering away from the door.

When we were sure they were gone, Eric and I scrambled out the fire exit. I threw myself in Eric's car and reclined the seat all the way back down to "therapist's couch" position until he rolled away and it felt safe to pop back up.

* * *

I don't think Dr. Carl ever put together that I was the nutcase in his fiancée's bathroom. And I never got the chance to come clean, because I never went back to treatment. I booked a very serious job on a SAG ultra-low-budget indie that landed me in nearby Sylmar for two weeks. And the demands of playing Wendy in *Ring Around the Rosie* were just too intense to juggle with grad school, so I dropped out.

In a way, I guess Dr. Carl was right. My learning that he was a normal guy who ate Jerry's Famous Deli sandwiches and would probably spend his honeymoon at a Courtyard by Marriott *did* affect the way I saw him. I couldn't continue to project my fantasies onto him. He wasn't my father, my fiancé, or my lover. He wasn't even my therapist anymore. He was just a middle-aged divorcé with reasonably good style and a car that wasn't the Mercedes E class I'd been trying to break into. Turns out, he drove the Hyundai with the COEXIST bumper sticker parked next to it.

4.

I Need Everyone to Love Me

I need everyone to love me. My feelings of inadequacy and lack of parental attachment have made me one of those sick bitches who can't tolerate feeling ignored. My parents say all the right things when they are pretending to listen to me. But the truth is, they are more like cats. They accidentally had a litter of kittens, and then emotionally moved on to whatever ball of yarn rolled past their line of sight. When self-obsessed people breed, they make empty people like me who spend the rest of their time on earth trying to gain the love and approval they didn't get as children. This doesn't excuse my behavior. It's just to say, if my parents had actually noticed me, I probably wouldn't care so much about whether everyone else on the planet adored me. Unfortunately, I'm a bottomless pit of need, and here are several people who have suffered because of it.

My Future Ex-Boyfriend

Before you meet the love of your life, there's usually one guy you date that you try to convince yourself is him. Let me save you some time: He's not.

In my early twenties, my friend Chad attempted to set me up with a friend of his from work. He explained that Lance and I were exactly alike in thinking we were better than other people, and we would no doubt have a million more things in common. I was intrigued. Chad typically hated the idea of me with any man. It took away from my time being the stand-in for his out-of-town girlfriend, Erica, who was dating another guy, not returning his phone calls, and in no way considering herself his girlfriend. I knew if Chad was willing to doff off his plus one, this guy must be worth it. So I agreed to meet him.

After a few days of silence, I called Chad.

"What the fuck? I thought you were setting me up with my soul mate?"

"Yeah. Well, turns out he's dating someone and it just kind of got serious."

"So, a week ago he was willing to be set up and now he's in something serious? I don't get it."

"Well, he bought her a Christmas present," Chad explained. "He said he'd still love to hang out as a group one night, though."

Eww. Fuck this guy. He thinks I'm fucking desperate enough to go out under the pretense of "hanging with a couple of friends," just because I *need* to meet him?

"Tell this guy to eat a hundred-calorie pack of dicks. Also, I'm really offended you would think I'm anything like this douche."

"What do you mean? Meeting someone while you have a boyfriend is totally a 'you' move. You're like the queen of the unintentional date."

I hung up on him.

It was true. I'd often found myself having coffee or dinner or a weekend away with someone who, I'd learn over the course of conversation, thought we were an item. I'd done this with neighbors, stepbrothers, people sitting next to me on airplanes, and even my college guidance counselor (who did help me graduate in less than three years).

Chad had a point. In fact, maybe Lance *was* the male me.

For the next two months, every action I took was a strategic move to make Lance, whom I'd never met, throw himself off a bridge. I couldn't believe I'd been rejected sight unseen. We never even spoke on the phone. He had no knowledge of my love of German literature, my eclectic taste in music, or that I was able to do a one-handed back walk-over. According to my father, whom I still kissed on the lips, I was the catch of the century. I was a goddamn debutante, and this fucking guy thought he could just pass on ever knowing me altogether? It made no sense.

I hope he dies in a grease fire, I thought.

Six months later, Chad called me from work. Lance was apparently single now and suggested the three of us go out to dinner.

Well, well, well. Look who decided to come crawling back. I told Chad I'd need to check my schedule and get back to him, then did a victory "fuck you dance" around my apartment.

"This is what happens when you play out of your league!" I screamed at the mirror before taking a dramatic swing at it and severely injuring my fist.

An hour later, I called back and agreed to a Friday night dinner.

When Friday rolled around, I started to get nervous. I knew I had to restore the scales of dating justice. There was too much at stake (my ego). I rummaged through my closet and changed outfits three times, but nothing seemed to work with my swollen elephant hand. Eventually, I decided to go with a pair of lace fingerless gloves I had left over from Halloween and a black sweater with jeans. I was aware that maybe my gloves looked a tad unconventional, but I didn't have much of a choice and what I lacked in style I vowed to make up for in personality. After all, my goal wasn't to date Lance; it was to make him spend the rest of his life wishing he'd dated me. He rejected me, triggering all my infantile feelings of worthlessness. Now it was time for him to regret it forever.

Walking into the Mexican restaurant Chad picked in West Hollywood, I instantly felt transported to the places in East L.A. that I lock my doors when I drive past. The restaurant was dark and dingy, obviously something Chad had a coupon for. Standing next to the Pac-Man machine in the corner was Lance. He was cuter than I expected in an awkwardly tall, total-dork-I-would-have-cheated-off-of-in-high-school sort of way. He had long shaggy hair that he tucked behind his ears and brown eyes that almost seemed too big for his face.

Lance saddled up to the machine to take a turn. His disturbingly long spider legs angled out on either side as he whisked the joystick around. He crushed level four. And five, and six, and seven. I realized I wasn't dealing with some cocky asshole who was going to try Neil Straussing me into fucking him. He was an actual, bona fide geek—maybe even a Rain Man.

"Hey, guys! Isn't this place great?" Chad said with an earnestness that made me wonder how we were even friends.

The three of us were escorted to a table in the back of the room. The dinner was innocuous and the conversation light. Lance talked a lot about manifest destiny and all the things he loved about Batman.

I drunkenly got fingered by my agent's assistant in an attempt to spite you, I thought to myself, watching him show Chad a wizard trick with his straw.

Once we finished, Lance asked if I could drive him back to

his apartment several blocks away. Reveling in the fantasy that he didn't have a car, I obliged. This poor, innocent fool needed my compassion. Sure, he was relatively good-looking and had a job far more stable than mine, but that was no reason for me to like him. I'd shown him that I was irreverent, engaging, and uninhibited, and now it was time for him to never see or hear from me again. Unless, of course, it was on TV and I was riding Brad Pitt naked in flattering lighting that didn't make my boobs look like penne pasta noodles.

When we pulled up to his place, he brazenly invited me inside. Taken aback, I agreed. Mainly just so I could rub my perfume all over his couch, pretend to be interested in his *Lord of the Rings* boxed set, and then leave him with the hug that would launch a thousand hard-ons.

His apartment was clean and sensibly decorated. Knowing I wasn't there to hook up with him, I didn't do my usual "excuse myself to the bathroom and make sure he doesn't have a Valtrex prescription" routine. Instead, I plopped down at his desk and started fucking with some sort of model spaceship he was building.

As he sat on his couch watching, I knew there was no way in hell he could resist falling in love with me from afar. And so, after accidentally twisting off the forward fuselage and crew cabins, I apologetically put his spaceship down and stood up to leave.

At that exact moment, Lance's home phone rang. His answering machine responded before he could.

"Hey, Lance, It's Kate. I'm just listening to the Strokes and thinking about how we used to fuck all the time to this album. I'm sooooo wet right now." *Beeeeeep.*

The fuck!? Did I just hear that correctly? My mind started spinning.

"I. Um. Wow. I swear I haven't spoken to that person in at least—"

I stood there flabbergasted for about thirty seconds, trying to process what I'd just heard before finally asking, "Who has sex to the Strokes?"

Bright red, Lance looked at me and shook his head, speechless. Like Pac-Man, he was backed into a corner. And so, sandwiched between the Ghost of Girlfriend Past and the Ghost of Girlfriend Future, he did the only thing he could do. With one of his long Inspector Gadget hands, he reached out and pulled me into an embrace.

My perspective on Lance had changed suddenly and completely. Before the phone call, he was a total geekbot. After the phone call, he was a stud—or, at least, he was someone attractive to someone other than me. That meant he had someone else to think about besides me, and *that* I couldn't allow. Passionately, I kissed Lance with my best "you'll never forget me" semi-tongue kiss.

Then, I must have fallen into some sort of K-hole, because it wasn't until a mortgage, two dogs, and four years of speaking Klingon later that I woke up and realized I was still dating Lance.

Unlike with Kate, Lance's ex—the one he passed on meeting me for, the one he bought Christmas presents for after being aware of my existence in the world, the one I'd found only one picture of on his hard drive—he and I sadly had little sexual chemistry. Neither of us could tolerate real intimacy. As a result, we were present with each other physically but absent emotionally. Our make-out sessions would devolve into shadow puppet shows on the walls. Our pillow talk would be about Alan Moore, artist Dave Gibbons, colorist John Higgins.

The relationship eventually turned into a platonic partnership. But for those few years, Lance was my closest confidant and best friend. He encouraged me to do things I never thought I could do, pushed me to conquer my eating disorder, and supported me when I had less than a few thousand dollars in my bank account. There were several times over the course of the relationship when I probably should have left, but my codependency, my fear of abandonment, and my genuine admiration for him prevented me from letting go.

My Future Ex-Boyfriend's Ex-Girlfriend

In the twilight of our relationship, I'd fallen into a bit of a depression, and my resentment toward Lance was mounting. Every time I wanted to address our issues, he'd shut me up and, like a good Catholic, insist there was nothing wrong. I knew I needed to end things, but instead of facing that reality, I just started painting things like this:

I picture you in a coffin.

One night, we went to a group dinner that Kate had also been invited to at a friend's house. I walked into the party nervous and wishing I'd had a professional do my makeup. Kate was sitting in the living room practically glowing. She was beautiful, charming, and ecstatic about meeting me. As soon as our eyes met, she jumped up and ran over. She handed me a package. I opened it to find a CD by the Strokes. Written in black Sharpie across the cover was a note: *Not wet anymore. Just mortified!*

It turns out, I was right about Kate's drunken stupor. She had no recollection of making the phone call and only learned about it later when Lance told her the story.

I spent the rest of the evening not with Lance, but gabbing it up in a corner with Kate. She was me, if I'd gone to law school and actually did something meaningful with my life. Something about having been with the same man made me feel especially close to her—like she and I had a shorthand that only people who'd had the same penis inside them could understand. Then, in a twisted champagne-induced moment of weakness, I confessed to Kate that I feared Lance wasn't the one. I wanted him to be so badly. On paper, everything about us made sense—perhaps too much sense. He was a writer and I was an actress. We both grew up in the Southwest. We both liked Brie.

But for all our similarities, we were very different people. He hid his arrogance behind a soft-spoken, shy exterior, while I just let mine hang right out in the open. He hated talking, never liked to leave the house, and still believed his childhood was perfect. I knew I was damaged and probably left the house to avoid getting too introspective and OD'ing on Xanax. For our entire relationship, I was under the impression that Lance was wrapped around my finger, but the truth was that he would have cut a hole straight through me if the job of his dreams were waiting on the other side. To be fair, I probably would have done the same, but I would have at least made incisions that were below his bikini line.

Though it didn't look like it from the outside, I picked a guy just like my father, who, as Chad originally promised, was a lot like me but more fucked in the long run. Kate urged me to be honest and gave me her phone number in case I needed to talk more.

I didn't call Kate, and I didn't say anything to Lance about my feelings for another three months. When I finally did, it was heartbreaking. After sobbing for an hour about how I was giving up on "us" and telling me nobody would ever love me like he did, Lance surrendered to the fact that I was leaving him. We spent the rest of the night lying on the floor, holding each other. A sense of peace washed over both of us as we wept and made jokes about the new *X-Men*. I promised him I'd name him anything but Lance if I ever wrote about him in a book. He promised the weird footprint I'd accidentally made on the stairs when the hardwood was being redone would remain in the house forever.

We tried to decide what to do with the dogs. Teets predated Lance and was obviously coming with me. But we'd just acquired a new "attempt to save our relationship" dog, Baby Jaguar. Lance begged on his knees to keep her.

"Please, I just—I can't lose her too," he cried.

So, in a lunatic fit of compassion, I agreed to let Jaggy stay with Lance. In my mind, I assumed I'd still be a huge part of both their lives. It wasn't like I was giving back my keys to the house, or our joint credit card, or his heart. I was just moving out and on with my life.

To be frank, I never really anticipated Lance getting over me ever. I couldn't even see how it was humanly possible. He was a shut-in with limited access to the outside world, and I was fun beyond words. Eventually, I thought I'd take it upon myself to find him a nice semiattractive woman and probably become the godmother to their children. But that was obviously way in the future. First he'd need a good two to three years to mourn my absence.

My Ex-Boyfriend's New Girlfriend

I physically moved out on a Monday. The following Friday, I stopped by the house in the early evening to pick up some more of Lance's things I felt he'd want me to have. Certain I'd be running into him, I rehearsed our exchange in my head on the drive over.

"Look, I will always love you. I just think we owe it to ourselves to be honest about the situation," I pronounced as I drove up Mulholland and bravely turned down our street.

I half expected to find Lance asleep on the couch covered in udon noodles, his own vomit, and a pile of our old Christmas cards. I vowed that if I saw any of his urine in Arrowhead bottles around the room, I'd promptly take back full custody of Jaggy and force him to get medicated.

The sun had completely set when I rounded the corner of our cul-de-sac. As I got closer, something caught my eye. There was a car identical to mine parked in the driveway. I pulled up next to it and got out to look in the windows. Inside I could see a Mentos wrapper and a single, solitary hooker boot. I had no idea whom the car could possibly belong to. I walked up to the garage door and punched in a code to open it. The slats on the door inched their way back to reveal an even greater surprise: Lance was not at home.

I walked in the house, and Jaggy came bounding out of

the darkness. She seemed to be trying to tell me something with her eyes, but I couldn't decipher what. I turned on some lights, and the two of us walked upstairs to the kitchen. There, I saw an opened bottle of wine and two glasses.

Lance was clearly on a date.

I grabbed my phone and furiously dialed my friend Cab, whom I'd used for a rebound fuck two days before. "I—I don't even know what I'm feeling right now," I cried. "I can't breathe. Seriously, I think you may need to call an ambulance."

"Why do you care? Just get out of there," Cab urged me, using a tone of voice that suggested I should swing by for another quickie.

"It's just a little soon for him to already be dating," I said, now going through his bathroom trash can, checking for used condoms.

"Do I need to remind you of all the reasons you told me you left this guy? And doesn't this kind of put me in a weird position?"

"Cab, he's literally moved on with his life in, like, a matter of days!" I pulled out a naked collage I'd made of myself one Valentine's Day and placed it delicately on his nightstand.

"You are being nuts. Come over and let's go to dinner." I could tell by his tone of voice that he meant "come over and let me try anal on you." And so, after forty-five more minutes of sabotage, I left the house to go hate-fuck Cab.

"You feeling better?" Cab asked me later, while gnawing on a postcoital Cliff Bar.

"Yeah, I'm good," I lied.

I spent the rest of that night alone in my apartment, trying to get some catharsis by painting a picture of a woman bleeding all over herself. Before I knew it, it was 8 A.M. and still too early to drive back to the house to confront Lance. The thing that upset me most was the fact that I'd spent the last week feeling sorry for him. He kept telling me how he hoped I'd change my mind about us, how he might be developing an eating disorder, and how he still pictured me wearing his mother's wedding veil. He even got me to fucking make a Sophie's Choice between my dogs! By 8:05, I was furious and already in my car, speeding up Mulholland.

When I arrived at the house, the mystery car was still there. This time I didn't bother with entering through the garage. I marched straight through the front door.

"Bubby? Hello?" I called out, feigning innocence and walking briskly toward the bedroom.

When I entered, I saw a blonde, not-as-cute version of me with weird eyebrows looking up from my side of our bed.

"Hi," she said awkwardly as Lance charged out of the bathroom in his Christmas pajama pants to intervene.

I eked out a hi before my macho exterior crumbled and I dashed out of the room in a cold sweat. Whatever harebrained schemes I'd been plotting seemed to vanish from my mind as I ran into the workout room (read: empty guest bedroom with a shitty treadmill) and tried to regain composure. It wasn't the visual confirmation of Lance fucking someone new that bothered me so much as the fact that he now had a part of his life that I had no involvement in. I felt like I'd just walked in on my father with another family he'd been hiding from me. (Thank God my real father had a vasectomy the minute he realized the shelf in the back of his convertible wasn't considered a legal seat for passengers.) My pain didn't stem from wanting to be the chick with weird eyebrows lying in our bed; it stemmed from feeling out of control and abandoned. In seeing Lance with someone else, I was being forced to accept that I no longer had any power. Lance wasn't going to die without me.

In fact, he was doing just fine. Up till this point, I'd managed to preserve all my exes, like a butterfly collection on the wall. Every one was color coded, with a needle through their hearts and a vague look of approval in their eyes. The relationships might have ended, but their love was forever frozen in time.

Just as I heard the front door shut behind the girl, Lance walked into the room.

"I wanted to tell you, but I was just scared. You know I'm not over you or us. It's been a fucking week. But it's just like you said, we have to accept that this is happening. This other person is good for me. She is helping me heal, and I really need that. I need company. You know I can't be alone without ending up covered in udon noodles and my own vomit." He tried to hold me.

"I just— I— Her eyebrows scare me and she was touching Jaggy—and—she's clearly seven to eight years older than me."

"Jenny, she is three years older than you and very sweet. She knows all about you. You and I are always going to be in each other's lives. It's all going to be okay."

As I left, I convinced myself that Lance was right. I even started to like the idea of him being with someone I wasn't remotely threatened by. I kind of couldn't wait to buy her something stylish and take her for a spa day, where we could reshape her brows and I could judge her naked. I always thought of Lance as a sort of father figure, so I decided to look at his taking a new mate as giving me a much-needed mother figure.

I spent the next month doing all the things I would have done if Lance and this new woman were my parents. I stopped by the house for mail, ate all the unwashed blackberries out of the fridge, and showered there when it was more convenient than driving all the way back to my apartment.

Then one day, without warning, I got a call from Lance.

He asked for my keys to the house and told me that we should stop speaking until Carmen, his now "official" girlfriend, was able to feel a bit more comfortable with the idea of all of us being friends.

"But, how am I gonna see Jaggy?" I asked, appalled at the idea.

"That's the thing. I kind of think it's best if you don't."

"If I don't see my own child? I agreed to let her live with you! This isn't fair to me!"

"Jenny, it's temporary," he said. "Carmen is insecure."

"Well, maybe you shouldn't have told her what I said about her eyebrows!"

"Jenny, I obviously didn't. She knows nothing about that. She hates you for other reasons—" He stopped and refocused. "My therapist thinks I need to cut you off."

"Cut me off? Your therapist said that? Dr. Shaw? I thought he loved me!" I made a mental note to write a scathing Yelp review of Dr. Shaw as soon as I got home.

"I have to do it, Jen." His voice was drenched in maturity.

Seething with anger and frustration, I went to the Ralphs and used our joint credit card to buy groceries for everyone in the store. Loading my car with cases of wine, crates of tampons, and a whole king salmon, I got a text. It read:

"This is my last correspondence. Let's touch base in six months. I love you always, Lance."

I stood in the parking lot as a wave of silent anguish washed over me. Despite my best efforts to stay completely connected, Lance was cutting the cord on our friendship.

Six months came and went, and aside from one or two logistical phone calls he made to me from work, we had no contact.

Despite the unwelcome change, my life had taken a major

upswing. I was busy traveling the world, working once every two months and tripling the number of guys I'd ever slept with. There was little-to-no time to focus on my ex-boyfriend-best-friend-pseudo-father-figure and his nonthreatening-new-girlfriend-who-I-was-convinced-would-love-me-if-she-knew-me. That was, until the unthinkable happened: I met Jason.

My Future Husband

I won't bore you with the details of how we got together right now. I still have a whole goddamn book to fill with shit. I can't give you *everything* in this chapter, so just relax!

For now, let's just say, I met him: the man that would change the course of my life forever.

On rare occasions, I'd think of Lance and wish I could share my newfound happiness with him. My world was flipped upside down and he was the only person who knew me well enough to appreciate what that meant. One night after Jason and I made a sex tape with the video camera Lance's mom gifted him for Christmas, I expressed my sadness about the situation.

"It's a shame because you guys would really love each other," I said, scratching dried semen off my navel. "What pisses me off the most is that I would never have left Jaggy had I known I was going to meet someone and get into something so serious, so fast. I really think we should just go up to the house and steal her back." I laughed, only half-serious.

"Yeah, and for shits and giggles, let's just take Carmen too."

"Totally, and then she'll see how cool we are and—"

He cut me off. "Jenny, I'm kidding. We aren't kidnapping anybody."

"But—"

"No."

"Like, not even in a fun way?"

"There is no *fun* way to kidnap someone. People don't like it. Ever."

I eventually ran this idea past Lance when we met for coffee months later. He agreed with Jason that Carmen would be hard-pressed to see the humor in being kidnapped; she wasn't even cool with the two of us getting coffee. Before we parted ways, I told Lance that I was going to marry Jason. I think he was shocked things were happening so fast, but was still able to be encouraging. The truth was, we both had new lives. My idealism about our eternal bond as friends was gone, as was his need to pretend things would ever be the same. They weren't. And that was okay . . . ish.

My Future Husband's Ex-Girlfriend

Lance's refusal to worship me from afar forever consumed so much of my time that I didn't get the chance to properly dissect Jason's ex until we were engaged. When I did, I discovered something startling and yet completely appropriate. Jason's ex was still in love with him and wanted him back. But she wasn't the only one. Jason's family wanted the same thing.

While Lance dealt with our breakup by shacking up with the bizarro me and not RSVPing to my wedding, Jason's ex—let's call her Baz—dealt with their breakup by spiraling into a mild depression. She made a Web series about how he broke her heart. She wrote blog posts about him. She even made sure to call his nephews on their birthdays (something I still don't do, because I don't care about kids' birthdays).

I eventually met his mother on a trip to the Biggs household in New Jersey.

"So what am I supposed to do with all these Christmas gifts I bought for Baz? We were extrememly close," she announced like a hormonal thirteen-year-old girl, refusing to make direct eye contact with me.

At first, I found his mother's attachment sort of charming. I knew I was the score of the century and that all parents love me, so I didn't mind indulging her anguish.

"I'd send them to her," I said earnestly.

Jason shot me a look.

"I mean, if someone had presents for you, wouldn't you want them? It's not like you got her a bunch of framed pictures of her and Jason." I plopped down next to her on the couch like we'd known each other for fifteen years.

Her body language said it all. She hated me. And the gifts were most definitely framed pictures of Baz and Jason.

From what I gathered, Baz was always clinging on to Jason for dear life. The circumstances under which they got together were traumatic, and Jason's white knight syndrome kept him in the relationship roughly two years too long. I have to assume that Baz knew it wasn't going to work out, because I don't believe people get sideswiped in relationships. It's always just a matter of what someone is willing to see and what someone is willing to ignore. I think we are all guilty of overlooking things if it suits our own agenda. But whenever we do, we are always setting ourselves up for disappointment.

So, as bad as I could have felt for Baz, I really didn't. She wasn't an idiot. In an effort to self-preserve, she overlooked the bad and embedded herself in his family. She was a "yes woman" who went along with anything Jason wanted (including his occasional desire to hit up a Chuck E. Cheese's on the way to LAX) and voiced concern only when he wouldn't let her move in with him.

"You know, only a woman who isn't secure with you would feel the need to kiss your mother's ass so hard," I told Jason as I tossed one of his mom's cats across the room like a Frisbee. I stared up at a five-by-seven of Baz and Jason's mom in Mouseketeer ears, still hanging above the mantel. "That seems healthy."

Jason conceded, shaking his head and rolling his eyes.

On the last night of our visit, Jason's older sister Holly pulled me into a coffin-sized laundry room to have a chat out of earshot of their mom. She sat opposite me and took a deep breath.

"I just had a baby so I'm really emotional right now," she started.

Not sure if she was going to offer me a joint or ask if I wanted to try her breast milk, I kept my mouth shut.

"I still talk to Baz," she confessed in a wispy voice that belonged on someone less than half her age.

"Okay." I was bummed she didn't have any weed.

"She knows you and Jason are engaged and she said that out of respect, she thinks it's best that she and I stop talking. I just can't imagine not having her in my and my children's lives. She knits us each a Christmas sweater every year. What do I tell the kids? She's just gone?"

She had worked herself into hysterics. If it weren't for the tears pouring down her face, I'd have thought she was joking.

"I don't know how to deal with this. Will I ever get to see her again? Does she know how much she means to me? Is she thinking about us—?"

I stopped her. "If I were her, I would do the same thing," I lied. "She is being mature. It's just a weird position for her."

"But what I had with her has nothing to do with you and my brother. It's just not fair for me to have to lose a friend in all of this."

"I'd say one day you'll be able to be friends, but my ex wants me to have absolutely zero contact with his family and I broke up with him, so, you know . . . You guys will probably never speak again. It's weird," I said bluntly.

Realizing she wasn't quite ready for such a heavy dose of reality, I switched gears.

"Oh, come on, you know you guys are going to be friends. This is all just temporary." I felt like I was walking an eighth-grade girl through her first breakup.

She went on to some rant about Jesus that I tuned out, and eventually let me out of the room.

What I gleaned from that weekend was that Baz was more than just a girl to these people. She was their perestroika. She represented a time when Jason was still not able to voice his own wants and needs. From childhood, his mother made him responsible for her happiness, an ever fluxuating ideal that was, for the most part, impossible to attain. When the money came, his older sister also looked to him for caretaking and security. Jason knew Baz was in love with him so he tried to do what he did with the rest of the women in his life—be the "good boy" and love her back. By forcing himself to be happy with Baz, Jason was also ignoring the growing need for boundaries within his own family. Breaking free from Baz symbolized his growing up. He was an adult and was no longer willing to carry anyone's happiness on his shoulders but his own.

I tried to stay out of most of it because, frankly, I had my own enmeshment problems to worry about. Also, Jason's family was all under five foot, so I knew if they tried to attack me, I could take them in a fight.

On the flight back to L.A., my thoughts were consumed with Baz. I realized I knew relatively nothing about her aside from the fact that she was the human manifestation of every issue Jason had had with his childhood. But there were other things I was still learning. Crazier things. Things I couldn't help but become completely transfixed by.

I cataloged the small details I'd discovered over the course of the last three days: Baz was married once. She'd lived in Peru. She hated traveling. She had an outy belly-button. She "danced" in college. She knew how to make seventeen different kinds of chili. She had a fake nose but no boobs. She was a painter but didn't believe in selling her work. She was half Asian but only admitted to her Jewish side. She once appeared in the background of an Old Navy commercial. Wore tiaras. Hated sushi. Only spoke in a baby voice in the bedroom. Never drank water with ice. And hosted an online radio show about cocktails made with Splenda.

Who the fuck was this chick? I thought as I looked over at my sleeping fiancé, silently judging the fuck out of him.

When we were back home, I decided I needed to do a more thorough investigation of this complicated-yet-fascinating woman. The first thing I stumbled upon (stumbled upon = spent hours scouring the Web for) was a Web series she'd recently made about Jason breaking her heart. The videos were roughly ten minutes each and depicted my soon-to-be husband as the biggest dickhead on earth.

Was I offended? Hurt? Concerned that I might be engaged to the biggest dickhead on earth? *No way!* This was the greatest thing ever. Unlike Lance and Carmen, Baz still thought about her ex and, by default, *me*! Sure, she seemed a little jaded. But I knew with time her anger would settle into commonplace obsession. I probed further and found entire blog posts dedicated to the topic of Jason and Baz. The posts were always signed "Anonymous," but I was able to trace them back far enough to find one signed, "Baz35." While Carmen's ego couldn't handle knowing my middle initial, Baz probably knew what color dildo I had (purple). More important, she cared!

Her *Dating Jason Biggs* became my favorite YouTube show. Sadly, I was unable to share this information with my fiancé, Jason Biggs, because he thought it was unhealthy.

There was another dynamic at play. This was the first time in my life that I was in a relationship with a famous person. What I didn't realize when we first started dating was that being with someone other people care about makes you feel like you are unimportant, worthless, and a total failure at life. Yet again, I was being forced to confront the demons in my head telling me I didn't matter. My dad introducing us to people as "my daughter Jenny and The Actor Jason Biggs" didn't help.

So I'd be lying/writing-a-fucking-lie-of-a-book if I didn't admit to feeling jealousy toward my husband's notoriety. Before I met Jason, I could walk into a room and know people were looking at me because I was dressed in the cutest outfit of all time. After I met Jason, I was just a random nondescript chick standing next to Jason Biggs who you hoped knew how to work the camera on your BlackBerry. All the free apple pie desserts and easily made dinner reservations in the world didn't make up for feeling utterly invisible and like my outfit didn't even matter.

Baz offered something I desperately needed at this particular juncture in my life (and perhaps always had): a fan. She was interested in me for me. She thought about me when I wasn't around. She appreciated pictures of me looking skinny. How could I not be drawn to her? Baz was providing me with attention. Sure, it may have been accidental attention and directed my way only because I was with Jason, but nevertheless,

I was on her radar. I was her boyfriend's new woman. In essence, I was his "Carmen" (minus the pencil-thin creepy eyebrows). Through Baz, I had the chance to do all the things Carmen should have done for me. I was thrilled to offer her my friendship, my compassion, and a chance to babysit my dogs if I ever left town.

"Jenny, I don't want us to have anything to do with this person," Jason said to me one night. "She's a part of my past for a reason, and that's where I'd like her to stay." He'd caught a glimpse of my Google history and staged an impromptu intervention.

A sloppy trail of Internet Movie Database comments made it increasingly obvious that Baz was watching my every move. For fun one day, I tried to imagine myself through Baz's eyes. Having never met me, she could only guess what I was like through press photos and MySpace. The two-dimensional me was so much cooler than the real me. She didn't bite her toenails or eat food out of the trash. She was flawless and bronzed, with no boob stretch marks or butt zits. Grooming my online image to suit Baz's liking became a full-time job. I took pictures of myself in my underwear, scoured iTunes for obscure songs that I felt pertained to our situation, and even refurbished quotes from Henry Miller to make them look like my own. I was starting to care about her as much as I imagined she cared about me.

In retrospect, I wish I'd had the discipline to stop there. I knew what I was doing had serious consequences. Whenever Jason confronted me about my online performance art for a target audience of one, I found myself lying. I'd promise myself I wasn't going to look her up, feel guilty about my misdeeds for a day, and then go right back to it. It was almost as if beating myself up somehow purged me of my sins. It only made me hungry for more. I started covering my tracks on the computer, and wearing fake eyelashes to Whole Foods on the off chance that I'd run into her. Objectively, I knew I could never live up to the me that I had helped her create in her head, but none of that seemed to quell my longing to meet her in the flesh.

Just around the time production started on a short film Lance asked me never to make—an uproarious romp about kidnapping Jaggy and Carmen ("Kidnapping Caitlynn" on YouTube .com)—*Dating Jason Biggs* had its series finale. I watched the last episode next to a sleeping Jason with the kind of stillness I typically saved for masturbating. In the final act, Baz's character declares that she is finally over Jason and ready to start her life again.

What. The. Fuck, I thought. I nudged Jason's sleeping body and screamed, "Quick! Honey! Do something cute! She's over you!"

The idea of Baz moving on killed my soul. It was even worse than Lance moving on. (And not quite as bad as my parents never loving me.) Who was I going to keep wearing cute outfits for? Who was I going to picture watching me run on the treadmill? Without Baz, what direction did I even have with my life? If a pretty actress falls in the woods and there's nobody obsessed with her, does it make a sound?

The next morning I changed my MySpace security options to "free for all" in the hopes of showing Baz everything she was missing out on. I figured if I commented on pages she was likely to visit, it was only a matter of time before curiosity got the better of her and she was staring at an eight-by-ten JPEG of me in a wedding dress.

For days, there was no sign of her. Overcome with feelings of rejection, I started to go insane. Baz was giving me little to no choice. Like Lance, she too was moving on, and that was unacceptable.

What happened to the good old days where after you broke up with someone, they still hung around and built IKEA desks for you and shit? I thought.

I had no choice. If I wanted her back, I *had to* meet her in person. She had been a really good stalker to me, and she deserved a stalkee who would fight for her. I was convinced that if she saw me, her fire would reignite and she'd love me again . . . or at least wanna look at my MySpace updates every day.

I started driving by her apartment with increased frequency. I'd never seen her outside, but knew she had dogs, so I'd make it a point to go during shitting hours. Still, there was nothing.

My morning ritual became: coffee, followed by e-mails, followed by a complete Internet sweep for Baz. We weren't friends on MySpace, nor did we share any mutual friends. When she and Jason broke up, she severed all ties. This fact alone told me she was more mature and less trashy than the Marilyn Monroe tattoo on her ankle suggested. It also told me I was going to need to up my game.

How do you up your game when you're already trying to bait an emotionally fragile Internet stalker? By luring her in with somebody seemingly harmless, who of course would be me in disguise.

I had to be smart. I needed someone credible, someone whom she'd instantly trust and someone who wasn't obviously affiliated with Jason in any way. After days of labor-intensive research, I settled on my agent, Sarah. Sarah didn't really understand her MySpace page, so, after several beers, she seemed fine with giving me her password to add a few friends for her. Since I'd deleted Sarah from my own friends, there was no way Baz would be able to make the connection back to me.

I watched Sarah's friend request sit in the "pending" category for a solid week before—EUREKA!

"Baz took the bait and added me!" I blurted out to myself in the middle of a movie starring people less attractive than me.

Chills ran up and down my spine. I did a cartwheel through the theater lobby (which garnered way less attention than I was hoping for). I was granted access to Baz's inner circle, and all my questions were about to be answered. Wanting nothing more than to get to my computer, I went straight home. I locked myself in the study and spent a solid two hours reading every inch of Baz's profile. I had so much insight into her mind, I started to think I knew her better than my husband ever did. I'd find myself watching TV or strolling through the mall, see a pair of leopard furry handcuffs and say aloud to myself: "Oh, those are *so* Baz."

We were the very best of imaginary friends. Then, one day, Baz posted a note to her MySpace page, asking if anyone had a large leather chair she could borrow for a photo shoot. I guess I was feeling particularly boundary-less that day because, as Sarah, I instantly responded.

"I do!" I sat in my chair killing myself laughing at how ballsy I was.

My diabolical cackle was interrupted by a notification in my in-box. I looked to see what it was.

Wha— Wait— No! Holy shit, Baz wrote back!

The note was short. It read: "Could I use it?"

Oh my God, Baz just spoke to me! I picked up the phone and called Sarah at work.

"Hey, so remember when you gave me your MySpace password and you made me promise to never use it for evil? Well, do you have any large leather chairs in your apartment you aren't currently using?"

There was a long pause on the other end of the phone before Sarah finally replied, "Actually, I do have one. *Why?*"

Sarah has a large leather chair! This is obviously meant to be.

I almost couldn't believe how everything was playing out. All the stars were aligning. The universe was conspiring for my success just like Joseph Campbell always promised it would.

"You have one? Great, because Jason's ex-girlfriend needs it for a photo shoot."

"I'm sorry, what did you just say?"

"What?"

"Jenny, did you make contact with Jason's ex as me?" I could hear her containing herself from screaming.

"She has a photo shoot, she's in a bind—"

Click. Sarah slammed down her phone.

I knew what I was doing was teetering on the verge of insane, but I couldn't stop. I was too close to meeting my soul mate's ex–soul mate to turn back now. In less than a week, I could actually see Baz in the flesh. I needed to devise a way to casually insert myself into the chair exchange. Maybe I'd jog down Baz's street just as Sarah pulled up, or maybe I'd ask Sarah to do the exchange at her place, where I'd be hiding in the closet.

I called Sarah back to present this option to her, but strangely her line went straight to voice mail. I took it upon myself to let Baz know she could use the chair. She, in turn, gave me all sorts of juicy details: her phone number, e-mail address, current employment status.

I then called Sarah back to apologize and delicately inform her that our plan was now completely green-lit. She picked up this time, quickly learning that when you're trapped with a madman with a gun, it's best not to point out that the pantyhose on his head are too sheer and you can totally see his face.

"Our plan worked!"

"*Our* plan?" she said.

"Well, more mine than yours, but I wanted you to feel included." I really am a great friend.

Reluctantly, Sarah agreed. I still don't know why. I like to think it was my compelling argument, but in reality I think she just wanted me to shut the fuck up and stop calling her. I told her she could bring the chair, and I'd sit in the passenger seat in a wig and bikini posing as her "eclectic cousin in from Uruguay for the weekend."

"No," she said.

We compromised. I agreed to hide in her trunk.

The morning of the drop-off felt like prom. Baz didn't want to meet till eight, so I had ample time to organize my attack. I went to the hairdresser, had my roots done, and even got my toes painted You Don't Know Jacques! gray. Technically, Baz wasn't supposed to see me at all. I'd be hidden under a blanket in the back of Sarah's SUV, but I was pretty confident that if I looked my best, my hotness would shine through anyway. Also, I fantasized about popping up and pressing my face against Sarah's back window as she sped away in an attempt to make Baz think she was hallucinating. I always try to look super hot in people's hallucinations.

The plan was for Sarah to hand off the chair, then launch into a series of casual remarks about how she thought they might have a friend in common: me. She'd then drop details about my relationship, my career, and my adventurous attitude toward sex.

Evil? Horrible? I swear I didn't mean it to be. I just wanted Baz's attention. And I would stop at nothing to get it back.

I positioned myself in the rear of Sarah's SUV so that I'd still be able to see Baz's face to judge how much older she looked than me. I also wanted to see her expression when Sarah, as instructed, disclosed my jeans size.

Sarah reluctantly stuffed me in the plush back section of her hybrid Lexus SUV, bitching the whole time that if I ever told anyone about this, she would break my face and ruin my career, which was like threatening to cut the balls off a dog that was already neutered.

Parked outside Baz's house, I could feel anxiety-diarrhea boiling up inside me. From the front seat, Sarah made phone calls and waited for Baz to show up.

"I'm hungry. This is annoying. I'm missing a screening," she bitched.

Roughly a half hour later, Baz pulled up.

"Sorry I'm late. This is so sweet of you!" she said.

I watched two legs move toward the right side of the car.

Then, standing there, her hip to my eyeball, I saw her. She looked like every picture I'd ever seen, except more eccentric. She wore these white furry yeti boots and a sequined beret. She had broad shoulders and a deep voice. Her hair was calico colored and her hands were rough and scarred, like she'd spent the last decade blowing glass. I tried to imagine my husband having sex with her, but I just couldn't get past the yeti boots. I guess

I wanted her to be softer, more vulnerable, broken. This didn't look like a girl who was destroyed over her ex-boyfriend. This looked like a girl with the self-possession to stab me in the head if she discovered I was watching her from the trunk of an SUV.

Sarah helped Baz pull the chair from the backseat as I tried to give off a glow from my spot under a blanket. They carried it upstairs to her apartment and slipped out of view. They were gone for roughly ten minutes before I started psycho-texting Sarah's cell phone.

Are you OK?
What is happening?
Did she kill you?

When Sarah did finally return, she got in the car and said nothing. As soon as we got around the block, I started in.

"So, what happened? What does her apartment look like? Did you guys talk about me? Please tell me you took a picture together!"

"Jenny, you need to move on."

"What does that even mean?"

"Get over her! She's completely over *you*."

Was this true? Was Baz totally over me? And if so, why?!

Sarah would barely talk to me for the rest of the ride home.

It took a few days of cooling off before she could discuss with me what happened that night in Baz's apartment. Jason did come up, but never by name. Baz just made reference to a really hard breakup. There was zero mention of her ex's new fiancée, or sleepless nights spent thinking about what her ex's fiancée looked like in lingerie. I almost believed Sarah was right. Maybe Baz had chosen the high road and moved on. For a minute, I contemplated the high road myself.

Then I decided that it sounded super boring.

There was no way I was gonna let Baz get away. We had something special and real. She was obsessed with me and I loved her for it.

A month went by and I drove past Baz's apartment twice a day religiously, hoping to catch a glimpse of her. Sarah, meanwhile, wasn't returning my phone calls and was being overly cryptic about her weekend whereabouts. Then one afternoon, I was accidentally CC'ed on an Evite to a wine party Sarah was throwing at her boyfriend's house. When I read through the list of attendees, I spotted Baz's name.

Sarah and Baz were friends now. And it was my fault.

"What the fucking fuck is this about?" I screamed on Sarah's voice mail as I sped past Baz's apartment, convinced I'd catch Sarah outside with an overnight bag. "You weren't supposed to befriend the mark! You were just supposed to hand off a fucking chair!"

They'd obviously forged some kind of sick friendship that I was completely left out of. My abandonment neuroses kicked into high gear.

"I'm coming to that fucking wine party!" I texted her.

Seconds later, Sarah wrote back, "No. You aren't. You are not invited. That Evite was supposed to go to a different Jenny."

"See you there," I wrote before powering off my cell in a fit of frustration. It was the first time someone had officially uninvited me to a party since that cunt Natalie Pierson tried to leave me out of her My Little Pony birthday party in second grade. (Her twinkle-eyed pony, Gingerbread, went mysteriously missing the next week. It was found hanging from the monkey bars the following morning, in an attempt to re-create the autoerotic-asphyxiation scenario I'd recently seen on an episode of HBO's *Real Sex* with my mom.)

The Evite said cocktail attire. I racked my brain, trying to think of the sexiest dress owned by anyone in my circle of friends, and decided on a slightly whorish D&G hand-me-down from my friend Simone. I spent the rest of the day staring at myself in the mirror.

Jason could sense something was off between us, but didn't know what. I was carrying around such a heavy load of guilt that it was almost impossible to connect emotionally. Every time he'd ask if I was all right, I'd try to deflect it by saying something like: "I just can't believe how partisan our political system has become," or "I was just thinking about how I'd totally kill myself if my name were Irene," or "How weird is it that Steve Carell didn't play the neighbor Steve on *Married . . . with Children*."

The truth was, my thoughts were consumed with Baz. The more I focused on her, the further I drifted from Jason. She was providing me with something he couldn't: a chase.

And just like that, I found myself cheating on my husband with his ex-girlfriend.

It may have been an emotional affair. It also may have been completely one-sided. Regardless, it was happening, and I didn't have the willpower to stop it. Yes, I felt like fusing with her initially subdued my own insecurities and somehow helped me absorb her power. But I also felt I owed her something. I got invested. I started to believe it was my obligation—to understand her in her own words, to hike Runyon Canyon with her, to help her come to terms with the fact that Jason married someone else and she was almost too old to have children.

The more fulfilled you are by one person, the harder it is to maintain intimacy with another. And the longer it's left unattended, the harder it is to come back from. Though I didn't see it at the time, my pseudo-relationship with Baz was subtly sabotaging my marriage.

I managed to get out of taking Jason with me to the wine party (by not telling him I was going to a wine party). When I walked in, Sarah was already tipsy and hanging off the side of her couch.

"She's not coming!" she shouted to me from across the room. "Didn't say why." She then slammed a fistful of Laughing Cow cheese cubes into her face.

Irritated, both by the fact that I wasted a spray tan on an event that didn't bring me any closer to Baz and that Sarah would serve Laughing Cow cheese at a party that required jackets, I left.

Somewhere between unclipping my hair extensions and devouring three thinkThin bars in my kitchen, I had a moment of clarity. I was being pathetic. Like, attending-a-social-event-thrown-by-my-agent pathetic. Baz wasn't reaching out to me in any way. In fact, she probably wanted nothing to do with me. I needed to be done.

The next day, I woke up with an air of "I'm married and Baz is dying alone" confidence. I told myself I'd wasted enough energy trying to gain the affections of my husband's ex and it was time to move on with my life. I kissed my husband extra hard, took in my amazing life, and tried to put all things ex-girlfriend out of my head. I agreed to meet my sister for lunch. Driving down Sunset, I had two options: turn down La Cienega to avoid Baz's apartment or take Crescent Heights. I took Crescent Heights. But only because La Cienega looked congested and Baz lived on Crescent Heights.

I drove with purpose, not expecting to see anything. At this point, cruising past her apartment was more ritual than obligation, and since I'd recently gotten off Zoloft, I allowed myself small compulsions. I must have stopped for a pedestrian or small child (they're not pedestrians yet), I don't really remember, because when I looked left, I was staring at Baz. She was finally outside her place, walking the dog I'd started to believe must just shit in a colostomy bag because it never left the building.

Without hesitating, I did a huge U-turn in the middle of the road and drove down the block after her. Knowing this could be my only chance, I rolled down my window, honked my horn, and called out to her.

"Baz!"

She spun around and instantly her face went white.

"I'm Jenny!" I called out, as if she'd just won the lottery.

She looked both ways, no doubt trying to decide which direction to run. But it was too late. I'd trapped her. She was going to have to interact with me whether she wanted to or not. I threw my car into park in the middle of the road and hopped out.

"Hiiiii!" I said as I went in for a hug.

Baz looked like a disaster. She pulled the hood of her jacket over her calico head as she explained that she'd just gotten back from a wild night in Vegas. I wasn't really listening, though, because I was too busy making a mental note of all her flaws in case I ever needed to draw a picture of her.

"I saw your photo in a pile of old stuff Jason and I were burning. . . . I was just driving through the neighborhood, looking another house for us to buy. You know, for our rental portfolio. I didn't realize you lived up here!"

"Oh."

"Well, I'd love to grab coffee sometime. I feel like we have so much to discuss. I don't know why I'm crying, sorry." I was tearing up the way I do after sex.

"Sure," she said, completely weirded out by the mascara dripping down my face.

"Well, what are you up to in like an hour?" I smiled and wiped snot on my sleeve.

"Ummm. Not sure. Can I . . . text you?"

"Of course!" I gave her my number as she backed away.

Two hours went by and I still hadn't heard from her. After lunch, I decided it wouldn't hurt to check in.

"Hey you, it's Jenny," I texted like we were best girlfriends. "Just wondering if coffee is still happening? I'm avail. Let me know."

"How do you have this number?" she texted back. "I didn't give you mine, just got yours."

Fuck. I'd forgotten the reason I had her number was because she'd given it to me when I was impersonating Sarah.

"Jason gave it to me," I lied.

"That's unexpected and cool, I guess," she wrote back. "Can you meet at Hugo's on Santa Monica around four?"

Could I ever! I'd have traveled to fucking Anaheim to sit face-to-face with Baz and her fake nose. This was turning into the best day ever.

Four P.M. rolled around, and Baz walked into Hugo's in a sundress and Doc Martens with so many leopard scarves wrapped around her neck, I thought she might be hiding a tracheotomy. She reminded me of a Betsey Johnson store circa 1993. I stuttered at first, trying to figure out where to begin, before accidentally launching into my history with Lance and Carmen. My hope was to disarm her, to sort of say, "Look I'm just like you—except engaged to the man you thought you were going to marry." On some level, it worked. I could see Baz wanting to hate me but at the same time being compelled to open up. Jason cut her off cold turkey, and I was like a crack dealer who had shown up at the end of her ninety-day rehab—just too hard to say no to.

She wasn't stupid. If, as I told her, Jason knew about our coffee date, he would no doubt be hearing about what was discussed. Baz regaled me with stories of her relationship with Jason, and I was riveted. The man she described was in no way the guy sitting at home, folding my laundry. She made him out to be a controlling, self-involved douche. Some of her tales had me cracking up, laughing, like the one about him not letting her put a hot pink pillow she liked on his sofa because it wasn't his taste. Others had me staring openmouthed in disbelief, like the one about him throwing a tantrum in Madrid because he was pissed at her for getting food poisoning. It wasn't like he ever beat her or did anything outrageous enough to warrant arrest. It was just obvious that he wasn't into her.

I left Baz that night caring about her more than ever. I tried to soothe her pain by saying things like, "Well, you both were young and he obviously had some shit to work out." And, "If it makes you feel any better, he is *nothing* like that anymore."

When I got home that night, I was sort of secretly pissed at Jason. He hurt my friend Baz. After dinner, I started asking questions.

"So, did you really leave Baz in Madrid one night because you were mad at her for getting food poisoning?"

"Did my sister say that?"

"Yeah," I lied.

"Come on, Jenny, really?" he laughed. "Do you know me at all?"

At this point, I wasn't sure I did. Baz seemed so cogent in her retelling, I didn't know what to believe.

"Baz was completely psychosomatic," said Jason. "Do you

have any idea what it's like to be with someone who is constantly ordering a wheelchair everywhere they go because they feel faint? Also, I told you I don't want to talk about her. Ever." He walked out of the room, slightly offended.

Just then my phone beeped with a text. It was from Baz.

"I had such a nice time today," she wrote back. "Let's definitely do something again."

By the tone of the text, it was clear Baz now wanted something from me. I wasn't naïve enough to believe it was just friendship. I'm not a fucking idiot. I was a gateway drug to her actual addiction: Jason. Through me she could not only find out what her ex's new life was like, but she could also work through her anger by telling me all the things she lacked the balls to tell him. If I were her, I'd have done the same thing.

As I was reading the text, Jason passed by. "Who's that?" he asked.

"Your sister."

"Tell her to stop talking shit," he said without stopping to make eye contact.

My heart was racing. Thinking fast, I shifted my cell settings into "shady bitch mode." I couldn't risk Jason picking up my phone and seeing a barrage of texts from the one person on the planet he didn't want me talking to. I already had her number listed under the pseudonym Professor Plum. But if he looked at the actual digits, he'd know it was Baz. My affair was no longer one-sided. I knew I was playing with fire, but my addiction to the attention outweighed all logic. I needed *more*.

Baz and I agreed to hike Runyon Canyon together the following week. Somewhere near the dog piss-covered park benches, my guilt became unbearable. I finally confessed to Baz that Jason knew nothing about us hanging out. I needed to talk to someone, and though she was the problem, she was also my closest confidante besides Jason.

"It's not that I don't want to tell him. It's just that . . . well, he thinks he hates you for robbing him of three years of his life and for being as nuts as his mother," I explained delicately, using the skills I assumed I would have learned had I not dropped out of psychology grad school. "Look, I know in time he will realize his anger is misdirected and that you only represent a time when he felt trapped on a myriad of levels, you know?"

Baz looked at me, incredulous, then called me on my bullshit: "If your husband doesn't want you seeing me, why are you doing it?"

I hesitated for a beat. The truth was, I didn't have a good answer. I mean other than that I was an empty shell of a person desperate for love and attention. But I figured she already knew that.

"I guess I'm here because I'm a healer. I like to heal people. I'm a healer."

For the next month, Baz and I continued seeing each other. The fact that she kept accepting my invitations to hang out, even after I admitted that Jason knew nothing about our relationship, told me she too was getting some sort of sick satisfaction out of the friendship. My assumption was that she liked knowing she had something on the guy who'd always had her by the balls. For me, it wasn't so much that I enjoyed hanging out with Baz, but more like I'd witnessed a car accident, and I couldn't *not* jump into the road and scream, "Clear the way, people! I'm a doctor's daughter and you need my help!"

She and I were night and day—we shared none of the same interests, and had little or nothing to talk about other than my husband. But that was enough. I knew it couldn't go on forever, and I justified my actions by constantly telling myself it was just a phase, something I needed to explore in order to put behind me. She started it, after all (except for the part that I started). If she hadn't shown signs of obsession, I wouldn't have been provoked. Besides, there was some good coming out of it. Every time I was around her, I felt great about myself! She helped me appreciate how good my life was.

I always paid for our meals and would joke whenever the check arrived that after putting up with Jason for three years, the least I could do was buy her lunch. Once, I found a box in the garage filled with things she gave Jason back during their breakup. The best part was that it was composed exclusively of gifts he bought her—as if forcing him to see the neon-colored trench coat and bedazzled Mousketeer ears was going to make him think better of his decision to leave her. I couldn't help but think that if I'd been in her life earlier, I would *never* have let her send a box like this to anyone. That said, I loved the box, and once I'd tried every article of clothing on to make sure it fit me loosely, I started systematically gifting things back to her. You know, as like a little treat.

As she drove us to Sheila Kelley's pole dancing class one afternoon, I whipped out a pair of Sam Edelman sandals and dangled them in front of her face.

"Remember these?"

Upon seeing the gnarled-up gladiators, Baz burst into tears. "I can't do this anymore," she whimpered as she slammed on the brakes and buried her face in the steering wheel.

Baz explained that the shoes represented to her the night Jason moved out. She'd lost her temper and kicked her foot through a skylight. Unsure how that was physically possible, I just nodded and held her hand in support.

"Maybe we've moved too fast with things," I said with sadness. "Maybe you need some time before we can have a friendship that isn't fraught with these kind of potholes."

"Or maybe we just can't be friends," she said.

I paused, feeling the sting of her words. But I knew deep down she was right. For the first time in my life, I wasn't doing the breaking up. And for the first time in my life, I was willing to accept the rejection. Baz had the courage to do the one thing I'd struggled to do my whole life: let go.

Baz dropped me off at my car and I went home. When I arrived, Jason was cooking and a few of my real girlfriends were sitting in the living room, watching him. In that moment, I realized how selfish I'd been behaving. For the six months I spent investing in Baz, my real life kept moving forward without me. I allowed my obsession to alienate me from the people I actually loved. My marriage should have been my top priority, but instead I focused only on feeding my insatiable ego. Jason deserved better than what I was giving him. And it was time to focus on *our* relationship, not mine and his ex-girlfriend's.

Like all addictions, banishing Baz from my thoughts took time. But eventually I did get to a place where she no longer consumed me. I called her when I heard her cat died. Jason and I once bumped into her at the mall. And I think I might have invited her to "Like" my Facebook fan page. But for the most part, she went back to where she belonged: the past.

5.

Show Me Your Teets

I've always assumed that people who don't own pets are serial killers. And post-college, I was in a pretty dark place. Not to the point where I'd ever be able to kill someone, but definitely in a place where I was listening to too much Morrissey. I'd spent the majority of my time at UCLA studying German literature, feminist theory, and mime. I was twenty-one years old and had just finished work on an adaptation of Kafka's *The Metamorphosis* where Gregor Samsa was depicted as giant labia. Needless to say, I wasn't in the greatest place emotionally. Then by pure chance, I stumbled upon a man who changed everything: Mr. Teets.

My sister, Amanda, was in college at Long Beach State at the time. One weekend I drove down to visit her. On my way, I got a flat tire. And although I wrote my thesis on the antiquated notion of a damsel in distress, I acted on my first instinct, which was to pull into the nearest gas station and start crying. A mechanic came out and told me replacing the tire would take about thirty minutes and that he hoped I could wait because I didn't really have a choice. I smiled the way you do at people who think they're funny but actually aren't and sat down to wait.

Directly adjacent to the gas station was a shitty pet store

with a sign outside that read POODLE PUPPIES 100 DOLLARS. Bored, I walked in and there he was, weighing three pounds soaking wet, the first love of my life. He was a ball of brown fuzz with blue eyes and tan markings around his face and chest. He was born January 30th, making him approximately three months old. I asked to hold him, and curiously, he wasn't nervous. The rest of the dogs seemed to be bouncing off the walls, trying to escape, but Teets was better than that, or he was on sedatives. Either way, he seemed confident and self-possessed. There was an instant, unspoken synergy between the two of us that I didn't feel again until I met my husband. We belonged together. After staring into his eyes for less than ten minutes, I bought him. (For the record, this was years before I knew better than to buy animals from a store, like some moronic Betty Draper type who smokes in the car with the windows rolled up while pregnant, then hands over a wad of cash to the proprietors of a backwoods puppy mill where dogs spend their lives locked in 3x5 cages. I would never make this mistake now. And so as not to endorse any future animal slavery, Teets has requested I lie and tell you he's a rescue.) I wasn't even looking for a dog. But just like with boyfriends, it's when you aren't looking that they always appear.

The most important thing to know about Teets is that, unlike most dogs, he's an actual person. I'm not one of those animal freaks who will tell you that all dogs are created equal. Some dogs are just dogs. Teets, however, is a person in a small dog-sized fur suit, and has to be treated as such.

When I placed him on the seat next to me in the car, he informed me with his eyes that he was both a gentleman and a scholar. He implied that he'd be willing to provide me with a lifetime of complete emotional support in exchange for a per diem of fancy meats and cheeses. Teets demanded respect—and a monogrammed suede doggie bed from L.L. Bean. It was a fair trade and a match for life.

I wanted to give my new significant other a name that matched his level of sophistication. He couldn't be something common, like Tiger or Barney. He needed a name with gravitas. Aside from looking like a young Richard Dreyfuss, there was someone else he resembled: John W. Teets.

The original John W. Teets was an Arizona business tycoon who was the retired CEO of the Dial Corporation. He was a mentor to my father and the one family friend who even as an adult I wasn't allowed to address by first name. I decided this regal toy poodle should command the same respect.

As a puppy-man, Teets was the model of elegance and class. I spoke to him only in German, but I think he picked up English from friends at the dog park. He insisted on drinking his water from a glass, and slept with his head propped on a Tempur-Pedic pillow. He never used a leash. He found them antiquated and offensive. He hated swimming but did enjoy wading up to his ankles in koi ponds, pretending to fly-fish like Brad Pitt in *A River Runs Through It.* Teets never believed in pants but occasionally donned a festive ascot or sweater vest when the mood was right. He was modest when using the restroom and pooped strictly in flower beds that could conceal his final product. He rarely misbehaved, and when he did, it was typically just a mutual misunderstanding.

For the most part, things were copacetic. And the two of us lived together in perfect harmony—until eventually, I ran out of money. At the time, Teets wasn't working and I was barely pulling in enough cash to cover his Fiji Water and organic bison chews. I knew downsizing meant our having to share a place with someone more financially stable but undoubtedly less snuggly.

The last time I'd had a roommate was my freshman year in college. Because I failed to turn in my housing application on time, I was condemned to a 150-square-foot, three-bunk dorm located on the only all-girls floor on campus. The dormitory opened up to new occupants on a Sunday. Knowing I needed to secure first dibs on the lesser of the three evil bunks, I wrote myself a doctor's note claiming that if I didn't move in the night before, I'd die of leukemia. My dad/co-conspirator signed the letter and changed the reason to something more believable. I think juvenile diabetes.

I woke up at 4:59 A.M. Monday morning to the sounds of my new roommate Hazel Buchheimer jimmying the dead bolt and barging in. The overachieving softball star from Greenwich, Connecticut, was horrified when she found me completely moved in and sleeping soundly on the top bed. I removed my sleeping mask and pretended to have diabetes until her parents were out of sight. About two hours later, Lupe Estevez, whom I referred to as Emilio Estevez for the rest of the year, marched in. She'd taken the bus up to L.A. from San Diego and was already pissed that both Hazel and I were white and owned cars. The friction among the three of us was palpable, and with time devolved into all-out war. Hazel started hiding food from us in her padlocked closet. Estevez reported me to campus police for streaking naked through the book fair. And I picked the lock to Hazel's food closet and framed it on Estevez. By the end of the year, none of us were on speaking terms. Except for when I think Hazel and Estevez would talk about me behind my back, and totally be on speaking terms. Traumatized, I vowed to spend the rest of my life living solo.

So years later, when my friend Indra's brother, Herschel, moved to L.A. and brought up the idea of moving in with Teets and me, I laughed. Hershel was an Orthodox Jew with zero hot friends and way too many Phish CDs. He was only two years my senior but already felt middle-aged because of his crazy beard. He worked in the world of finance while I worked in the world of taking cute pictures of Teets.

My limited income in those days came from tutoring. After college, I hooked up with a friend who ran a tutoring business and I agreed to help him out part-time by teaching English as a second language. Every week, he'd send me handfuls of eager clients hoping to improve their grammar and pronunciation, and I'd work with each of them for about an hour. The reality was, I had no idea how to teach English. But I did know how to speak it. *So how hard could it be?* A typical session at the Jenny School of Immersion would start with me making a pot of tea, requesting twenty bucks, then spending an hour overenunciating whatever thoughts and feelings popped into my head. If I had auditions, I'd make my pupil practice lines with me, then drill them on whether or not they thought I was believable. Sometimes it was hard not to feel guilty taking money from innocent people, but at the end of the day, Teets needed bison chews and I needed to memorize my lines.

After some serious thought, I warmed up to the idea of moving in with Hersh. I was an overeducated, unemployed actress, and the only man in my life was neutered. Herschel had a stable job, no sex life to get all over my linens, zero interest in stealing my clothes, and more than a little cash to spend on a killer pad. To top things off, his Jew 'fro sort of looked like a poodle, which made me feel safe. Us joining forces would mean less tutoring, a bigger apartment, and a hairdo that in the right light could pass for a brother figure for Teets.

Over time, Hershel got used to giving Teets commands in German and I got used to hiding my Canadian bacon in my car. We were like *The Odd Couple*. He was the pious, left-brained, mathematical genius who taught me how to tip at restaurants and never used a brush, and I was the right-brained artist who only went to temple on high holidays and exposed him to his first painting of a girl being unintentionally fucked in the ass.

Teets came to know him as *"der Uber Juden,"* and I simply thought of him as "the Chia pet in the master bedroom." Then, in early spring, an incident occurred that changed everything.

Amanda was in town for a day, so we decided to take Teets to The Grove, an outdoor mall on the east side of town, for some lunch and passive-aggressive bonding. Teets trotted along beside us as we tore through Forever 21 with the desperation of women over twenty-five.

Now weighing in at a whopping nine pounds and eleven ounces, Teets was too big to hang around my wrist in a rainbow-colored Louis Vuitton. Also I wasn't Asian, so I didn't own a rainbow-colored Louis Vuitton. Instead I put Teets on a leash to ensure we wouldn't get separated and went to work trying to out-shop my sister.

The only problem with having a dog is that they often attract kids. I was in the middle of explaining to Amanda that a size 2 at Banana Republic actually means you are a size 6 in the real world when a little British girl jumped out of nowhere and started strangling Teets.

"Mommy, look at the puppy!"

Teets looked up at me for help while I answered the typical

series of non-dog-person questions. The red-haired four-year-old hung on to her mom's thigh and stared at me like a demented Chucky doll.

"He's two. Yup, a poodle. I know, he has human eyes, right? I kind of consider him a little man in a fur suit! Hahahahaha." Out of the corner of my eye, I caught Amanda forcing a saleswoman to undress one of the mannequins in the window. Amanda was going to get the last BLONDES HAVE MORE FUN baby-T in the store if I didn't act fast! Yanking Teets away, I started to walk.

"What's coming out of his bum?" The little girl pointed, nonplussed.

I turned to Teets and saw what looked like a shit-strangled condom drop between his hind legs. He had been trying to pull himself out the door to a nearby pot of ivy but couldn't because he was tethered to my side.

"Ewwww!" Amanda screamed across the store like a prepubescent boy in a sex ed class.

Before the mother could usher her daughter away, a second condom peeked out of Teets's winking asshole. This one, however, wasn't going anywhere. Teets was overdue for some manscaping, and his excess hair seemed to somehow tangle itself on the rubber, preventing it from falling. Amanda started to hyperventilate. I picked Teets up and shook him vigorously, but the prophylactic poop was going nowhere. Within seconds, a small crowd of shoppers formed around us like we were those living-statue street performers.

Seconds later a manager walked over. "Ma'am, we are going to need you to leave Forever 21 forever."

"She's not beating him. This isn't abuse! There's something stuck on his fur," Amanda assured both the manager and the crowd.

"Whatever it is, we'd like it outside. We're a Christian company."

I ran outside and held Teets over the closest trash can I could find. Amanda followed.

"Just so you know, everyone at this mall thinks you're the biggest slut right now."

"I don't even have boyfriend!" I said.

"Sluts usually don't."

"Just— Will you hand me a receipt or something so I can pull the rest of this out of him?"

Amanda rummaged through her purse but found nothing. Thinking fast, she ran over to the ivy and uprooted a fistful.

"How about a leaf?"

Having no choice, I folded the flaccid vines in half, turning them into makeshift tongs. Still holding him over the garbage can, I then took a deep breath and gingerly extracted the digested latex from my dog's sphincter.

Teets looked at me, mortified.

"Walk along, folks, nothing to see. She's not throwing him in the trash. Just doing some grooming." Amanda continued chattering out of nervousness, even though there was no longer a crowd.

It was the first time in Teets's life that he'd gotten himself into such a bind that rolling over on his back and flashing his penis couldn't get him out of. He knew that I knew that he knew better than to eat semen, especially when that semen didn't belong to anyone I was fucking. But he was his own man. I wasn't privy to his every move.

I had no idea where he could have stumbled upon a stomach's worth of Trojans. Was Teets a drug mule? Did he have AIDS ? Why didn't I have a boyfriend?

We drove to the vet, where Teets was X-rayed and a final condom was discovered in his intestines. The doctor prescribed some laxatives and told me to call if I didn't see number three in Teets's number two later that evening. He assured me that the problem wasn't behavioral and that Teets wasn't involved in any sort of underground drug ring.

"Semen is a salty and delicious snack in most dogs' eyes," he said. "He'd do the same thing if he came across a T-bone steak. Just instinct."

I was picturing my vet cumming into Teets's mouth when Amanda nudged me to hurry up. She needed to get home and we had driven in the same car.

Amanda dropped Teets and me off at our apartment and thanked us for a memorable day. When I walked inside, Hershel was standing in the hallway, holding one of my bathing suits. I was too weak to mention how the perks of living with a man were supposed to include my clothes going untouched. Instead, I said nothing and proceeded toward my room.

"I was just returning this because Olivia needed something to wear in the hot tub," he said guiltily.

In all the years I'd known Hersh, I'd never heard him mention females. I'd started to believe his faith prevented him from engaging with them, like shellfish. Hersh's awkward demeanor had only two possible explanations: He was either ashamed of being in the hot tub with a woman, or he *was* that woman. The latter seemed easier to believe.

"No worries," I said, making a mental note to tell Hersh he ought to reconsider Olivia as a drag name. He needed something more fitting, more personal. Perhaps Penny Pinscher.

"She's still here. Wanna meet her?"

"Like she's with us right now?" I looked around the room, hoping to catch a glimpse of Hersh's drag spirit guide.

"Umm. Yeah." He looked at me perplexed as he walked back into his room.

I took his leaving the door ajar as a sign for me to follow.

As I peered around the corner to the en suite bath that was costing Hersh an additional 150 bucks a month, I saw a woman on all fours. She looked like Hershel but not enough to be his drag alter ego.

"Someone got into your trash," she called out, continuing to Windex the floor.

I knew what had happened and I didn't like it. Hershel was having sex, and my dog was reaping the rewards. It was like Teets was Augustus from *Willy Wonka & the Chocolate Factory* and Hershel's trash can was a chocolate river, only it was actually filled with jizz.

Hershel tried to introduce me to Olivia, but before he could, I turned to him and unloaded the frustration of a day's worth of cleaning awkward dumps.

"Teets has been eating all your used condoms. Is it kosher to swallow? Because I think that would really help all of us if she would." I extended my hand to Olivia and smiled. "Nice to meet you, by the way. Oh, also you two aren't cutting a penis hole in any of my good sheets are you?"

Later that night, Teets hatched Hershel's final sperm baby and I went through my phone, looking for someone I might be able to reconsider as a boyfriend. Unfortunately, nobody compared to Teets. Regardless of the semen slurping, he was still a total catch with perhaps even stronger nails and better skin than before.

As time went on, Teets did eventually have to share me with other men and the occasional woman. But nobody lasted long until I met my husband.

When Teets first met Jason, he was cordial. Each time Jason came over, Teets greeted him with a perfunctory tail wag, and whenever Jason got near the bed, a look that said, "Don't fucking think about it." Teets never saw himself as stepson material. As good as Jason was at giving butt scratches, Teets still considered him an outsider.

Nine months later, Jason and I were married and Teets gained not only a dad but also a brother. Jason entered the relationship with a bit of baggage. Which is a nice way of saying, he had an asshole miniature pinscher. Harry was a three-year-old uncivilized dick who controlled Jason almost as much as his mother had. Unlike Teets, Harry demolished shoes, barked at inanimate objects, and took giant shits wherever he thought you might walk barefoot. Because of our vastly different experiences, Jason and I didn't always see eye to eye on how the boys should be cared for. I believed that Teets should have his own seat at the dinner table and that Harry should be taken out into the backyard and shot.

At home, it was easy to get away with customizing each dog's routine (Teets in bed, Harry in the canyon wrapped in bacon), but when we traveled it was a different story.

In my single days, Teets and I had our flying routine down pat: I'd look all doe-eyed and vulnerable while he'd don a SERVICE ANIMAL vest and escort me straight through security. We'd board the plane in front of the elderly and always sit by the window. When my food tray was up, Teets slept on my lap, and when it was down, he requested the cheese plate. My behavior appalled my husband for several reasons. The main reason being that he is a total rule-dork.

Jason is the type of guy who uses his blinker every time he makes a left turn on a green arrow. And he's the only guy I know who's never returned anything already worn to Nordstrom. He plays by the book and obnoxiously expects me to do the same. His other problem is that he is a celebrity and hates being seen getting preferential treatment. Once we were married, he made me promise I'd make a more concerted effort not to pretend to be blind, deaf, German, an English tutor, or diabetic just to make my life easier.

As a gesture of love, I did something I rarely do. I compromised. We were headed back East for Christmas, and both dogs were coming with us whether I liked it or not. Jason didn't want me lying about having a therapy animal, and I didn't want to spend three hundred bucks to not even be allowed to have Teets sit on my lap. To be honest, I felt like the airline should be paying *me* to have Teets on board. He was a joy to be around, a spreader of light and goodwill. So I made Jason a deal. If he helped me smuggle the dogs on the plane, I'd keep them hidden in their carriers the entire flight and never make mention of the fact that Teets was a "working dog" or that I was mentally ill. I assured him that he didn't need to buy the dogs tickets, because that just leads to more questions about paperwork I didn't have. If we did things my way, nobody would ever know they were there, he wouldn't have to deal with any weird looks or whispers, and our journey would go off without a hitch. Reluctantly, he agreed.

The four of us were scheduled to take a red-eye out of LAX. Before leaving the house, Jason fed Harry his tranquilizer, and by the time we were going through security, he looked like a drunken Janice Dickinson. Just before boarding, Jason stuffed Harry into a carrier. I put Teets in a matching carrier and planned to transfer him onto my lap once we took off. I tried explaining to Teets that only service animals are allowed to be out during flight and since Jason wouldn't let me use the therapy vest, he had no choice but to remain hidden under my blanket, like a third boob or a weird stomach pooch. Teets was offended but too gentlemanly to argue.

Once we were midair, I reclined my seat, popped an Ambien, and pulled Teets out of his carrier by his head like I was delivering a baby. Teets settled happily into my lap after taking a moment to passive-aggressively step over Jason's ball sack. Jason scowled at me, but he held back any objection.

Natalie Portman was about to tell Ashton Kutcher she wanted to be *Friends with Benefits* when I passed out. Roughly four and a half hours later, I woke up to a tapping on my shoulder, presumably preparing me for landing. I opened my eyes to see Jason staring at me, panic-stricken.

"Where's Teets?"

I looked down at my empty lap. The blankets I'd cocooned in earlier were strewn across the floor, and Teets was nowhere in sight. I quickly peered into his carrier. It too was vacant.

"Do you have him?" I asked groggily.

"Umm, no, Jenny, I *don't* have him. I *never* had him. Where the fuck is he?" Jason stood up and looked down the aisle.

"I should never have let you put him on your lap. . . ." Muttering to himself, Jason walked down the cabin toward the bathrooms.

I opened Harry's carrier to see if maybe Teets was inside with him. Harry sat up, hungover. He was alone. I then hung my head between my legs to check if maybe Teets was crawling under my seat. Again, I saw nothing.

Like the cutest snake on a plane ever, he was missing. I tried to put myself into his state of mind, reminding myself that he was more person than he was dog. The only reason people get up in the middle of the night on an airplane is to pillage a free Bloody Mary off the drink cart or to meet a hottie in the bathroom for a mile-high quickie. I rushed to the lavatory, which was OCCUPIED, and pounded on the door.

"Teets! Are you in there? Are you with someone? Can I come in?"

A dude who looked like Joaquin Phoenix during his nervous breakdown stumbled out. I looked into the bathroom. No Teets.

Jason came back fuming and rang the flight attendant buzzer.

"You're talking!" Jason reclined his seat and pretended to be asleep.

Seconds later, a Tammy Faye Bakker–looking stewardess appeared out of the darkness. "How can I help you?"

I looked back at my husband, who began fake snoring.

"Ma'am?" the flight attendant continued.

"Yes. Uh—I seem to have misplaced something."

Before I could finish, Jason shot up and started tattling on me like some grade school hall monitor with a fanny pack full of detention slips.

"My wife can't find our dog. We snuck him on the plane, and now he's missing!"

The flight attendant looked down to see Harry humping my discarded pillow like it was Jodie Foster in *The Accused*.

"Oh, not that dog. Another one," I explained.

Jason looked at me, speechless.

Armed with flashlights, the three of us moved from seat to seat. Thirty-seven aisles and six mini bottles of Jack later, we had nothing.

At four in the morning, just above Newark, the pilot intervened. He came on the loudspeaker and gave a vivid description of our runaway mammal. People were instructed to check their laps, look under the seat in front of them, and to please remain calm. The passengers were assured that the animal was nonaggressive, hypoallergenic, and bilingual.

"Found him!" a boy cried out over the announcement. Teets was raised up above a window seat only three rows back.

He had a piece of cheese hanging from his mouth and, luckily, no condom hanging from his ass.

"I'm gonna kill you," Jason exhaled, relieved.

The stewardess retrieved Teets and handed him to Jason while the rest of the passengers silently judged the fuck out of us.

"Aren't you Jason Biggs?" a guy looked up from his seat and asked.

Tammy Faye gave Jason a once-over. It *was* Jason Biggs!

And Jason Biggs was *not happy*.

Thinking fast, I did the only selfless thing I could think of. I threw myself on the ground and faked a series of convulsions. Jason's eyes bulged out of his head, horrified.

"I need my medication!" I moaned.

Eager to distance himself from the TMZ headline PUPS ON A PLANE, Jason backed away slowly. I dragged my gyrating body towards one of our carry-ons and whipped out a pill bottle. Tammy called out to a fellow flight attendant to notify the cockpit. Having no concept of how long it takes a person to stop seizing, I swallowed a Benadryl and stood up immediately. Reaching my hand into the side pocket of Teets' carrier, I pulled out his PLEASE DON'T PET ME, I'M WORKING vest and waved it in the air like a white flag. I explained to Tammy that Teets wasn't a stowaway but my trained medical aide.

"And who's that?" she asked, pointing to a postcoital Harry.

"His assistant."

She gave me a skeptical look. In response, I started acting dizzy and buried my head in my seat. I heard a voice come on the loudspeaker asking for a doctor, but none of the passengers replied. The second flight attendant ran back and whispered something in Tammy's ear.

"It appears that you're 'sick and in need of medical attention,'" Tammy said mechanically, still studying Jason's face like he was a mannequin at Madame Tussauds. "There's a flight backup at JFK, and we're currently twelfth in line to land. The pilot spoke to the control deck, and we have two options based on how you're feeling: We can wait in line about thirty minutes and take our chances, or we can tell them we have an emergency and move to the front of the line."

I already knew Jason's feelings on cutting in line, so I didn't bother checking in with him. "It's fine. I—"

Jason put his wrist to my forehead like he was taking my temperature and finished my thought for me. "I think we better land."

The cabin's hatred gradually turned to empathy and a request for a handful of signed cocktail napkins. I disembarked from the plane feeling proud of my husband for lying to get us out of an hour's worth of doing circles in the sky. Unfortunately, I knew saying that would only piss him off. I still owed him an apology. Once in the car and safely on our way into the city, I told Jason that I was sorry for the entire situation and any embarrassment he might have felt. I admitted that he was right all along and that there was only one person to blame. And that person, obviously, was Harry.

6.

The Birthday Whore

Thoughtful gifts can be so challenging. Especially for a spouse. There are anniversaries big and small. The holidays, real and Hallmark. And there are birthdays . . . every year. Fucking birthdays.

My husband and I were married for about sixteen months when I ran out of birthday present ideas for him. After several failed outings to the mall, I decided a hooker just made the most sense. I knew it wasn't something he already had, it wasn't something he was going to buy himself, and if everything went according to plan, it wasn't something that would end up stuffed in our basement for the next four years.

Besides, I wanted to do something sexy, something dangerous. Something to remind him that even though I sleep in tattered, period-stained boxer shorts and zit medicine most nights, I'm fun and exciting and capable of turning him on the way I did when we first got together.

I don't have any real role models when it comes to maintaining a relationship spanning more than a few years, or experience holding someone's full attention when I'm not constantly doing something outrageous. A hooker was so wrong that it just felt right.

I went to my phone and e-mailed my friend Cassie.

Being a talk show host, I knew Cassie was exposed to all sorts of freaks. She'd met heads of state, bearded ladies, monkey trainers, and even Candy Spelling. Even if she didn't know somebody willing to accept cash for sex, I was certain she wouldn't judge me for asking.

"Do you know any masseuses who will also fuck, etc.? P.S. Great show last night. So glad they're no longer dressing you like you live in Ann Taylor's Loft," I wrote.

Cassie replied instantly with just the name "Becky" (clearly a daytime pseudonym to cover up her prostitute-y name, no doubt something like Chardonnay) and a phone number. Ten seconds later, I called "Becky," explained the situation in vague terms, and asked if she could come over that night. She agreed.

Unable to sit on the surprise that awaited him, I ran into the bedroom to break the news to Jason.

"Baby, do you like hookers?" I whispered sweetly as I pounced on him.

"Like them? Like how?" he asked, distracted by his iPad.

"Like one is on her way over here right now to have sex with us!" I proudly exclaimed.

Jason looked at me, laughed, and went back to Googling images of himself.

"I'm serious! Becky is on her way. You need to shower and Vagisil your ball sack!"

The mere mention of his Vagisil addiction jolted him back to reality. He knew I was serious.

"Wait, a hooker is coming over? Why? How did this happen?" I watched him pretzel himself like a Chinese acrobat in order to test his current ball scent.

"It was supposed to be a surprise for your birthday, but I couldn't hold it in, sooo—"

He cut me off, which was good because there really wasn't

more to the story. "Jenny! A hooker? This isn't the kind of thing you can just spring on me! The house is a mess."

"She's a hooker, I'm sure she's open-minded," I assured him. "Don't you think it will be kind of sexy and different? We don't have to let her see upstairs if that makes you feel better."

"I guess," he said. I watched him gradually come to terms with his new reality. He exhaled. "Okay," he reluctantly agreed.

And so, around eight, I set the mood. I turned on a Buddha-Bar CD and opened a bottle of Dom while Jason paced around the house, sweating.

"Now, listen, I don't want to fuck her, because I don't want to get AIDS," he said. "But maybe I could just watch her go down on you?"

"On me? So you're fine with *me* getting it?" I appraised my body in the hallway mirror, thinking about how much skinnier I'd be if I had AIDS.

"Look, she doesn't have AIDS," Jason tried to assure himself. "She'll go down on you while you go down on me."

"That sounds like a lot of coordination for me. You know I'm left-handed." I was already buying a new AIDS wardrobe in my head.

When Becky arrived at the proper whoring hour of 9 P.M., I opened the door in a see-through bra and undies and led her upstairs to the bedroom. Becky seemed unfazed by my getup, which made me instantly regret not opting for something crotchless. She was more athletic than I pictured her, as I never like to imagine people in better shape than me. She had short dark blond hair and struck me as one of those chicks who, even if she's in a cocktail dress, wears zero makeup. I guessed she was around thirty, but in the right light, she could have passed for fifteen. I couldn't tell if she was gay or straight but for the sake of my ego, I pretended she was gay.

Jason appeared in the doorway several minutes later with the bottle of Dom and three glasses.

"Who wants to go first?" Becky asked earnestly.

"Oh . . . We can't go *together*?" I said suggestively.

"Well, I only have two hands."

"I have two, too," I offered seductively.

Rather than a sexy come-hither-let's-do-this-thing look, Becky's expression was quizzical. Puzzled. She asked me to undress and lie on her table facedown before excusing herself to the restroom. The minute she was gone, Jason shot me a look.

"She seems kind of legit," I said, hoping to distract him.

"Jenny! She's a masseuse! A literal masseuse! Literal masseuses don't have sex with you!" He downed his glass of champagne, then mine, and left the room.

He was right. Becky turned out to be an actual masseuse. (Real name: Becky.) She proceeded to give me a professional, non-sexual massage, all the while helping herself to the rest of the Dom.

"So many people assume that just because I'm a masseuse, I'm down for sex," she slurred. My massage was complete and Becky followed me back downstairs, wasted. "Can you believe that?"

Yes! I thought. *I am one of those people!*

Jason made up some excuse about why he was going to pass on his rubdown and insisted he'd take a rain check.

Becky plopped down on the couch and kicked her feet up. Though I didn't see her ingest anything else, her ability to form sentences continued to decline rapidly. She was so inebriated, I assumed she normally drank only noni juice or was maybe on Wellbutrin.

"You guys are soooo cool. I get so many douchebags in my line of work. We should hang out sometime. My boyfriend wrote a pilot you'd be perfect for." She pointed at Jason's nose like what she was saying was meant only for his nose to hear.

After deliberating through eye contact and subtle gestures, we (me, Jason, and his nose) decided the best course of action was to call a cab, then lure Becky to the front door and lock her out of the house. She protested at first, banging on the windows and screaming for her car key. But once we turned all the house lights off and pretended nobody was home, she got in the cab and left. After she'd gone, I packed her massage table into her van and left her key chain on the window in an envelope with her tip.

Once the smoke settled, I turned the lights back on and called Cassie.

"The whore you recommended *sucked!*" I screamed.

Cassie was in the middle of a dinner party and was laughing so hard she could barely keep the phone to her ear. "She isn't a whore, you idiot!"

"Yeah, I gathered that!"

"What happened. Tell me everything." Cassie put me on speakerphone so the rest of her party could revel in my misery.

"I'm gonna save it all for her to tell you. She's wasted in a cab, and the driver has your address. Bon appétit!" I hung up before she could respond.

The next night, I was not only pissed off that my husband's birthday treat hadn't come to fruition, but also deeply ashamed that I didn't have any friends with access to whores. I cried into my pillow before bed.

Jason tried to comfort me by reminding me that I didn't have that many friends. He also reminded me that we would be in Vegas the following weekend for his friend's surprise birthday.

"If you still want to do it, there will be more than enough opportunities in Vegas."

With Sin City on the horizon, I mitigated my inner rage. I'd pick up where I left off the second we landed.

That weekend, as soon as our plane hit the tarmac, I was on Cityvibe.com, trolling for escorts. I quickly homed in on a photo of a thin brunette with elbows for boobs and made the call.

"Hello?" a cutesy voice chimed.

"Hi, um, Eva? My husband and I are in town tonight, and we were wondering if you could get together with us?" I whispered, staring across the aisle at an elderly woman using Purell on her lips.

"Sure!" Eva enthused. "What time were you guys thinking?"

"How about four?"

"Sounds good. Why don't you call me when you get to your hotel, give me the room number, and I'll be there."

We checked into the Four Seasons under the name Drew Peacock. There were about fifty people in town specifically for the surprise party, and Alan, the birthday boy, wasn't to have a clue. On our way up to the room, I texted Alan's wife, Gertrude, to notify her of our arrival. She wrote back that they were in staying in 3512. They were heading down to the pool shortly.

"Shit!" I screamed, pulling my husband into an emergency exit stairwell. "We are in 3511!"

Not only was this logistically problematic, but it also complicated our afternoon rendezvous. From the stairwell, we peered into the hallway and waited for Gerty, Alan, and their two boys to disappear into the same elevator we'd just gotten out of. Once the coast was clear, we ran to our room and locked the door.

After a long and thorough shower, I started flat-ironing my hair and shooting minibar bottles of Grey Goose like I was going to prom.

"Do whores prefer eyeliner or just mascara with a pinch of shadow?"

"Maybe a smoky eye," Jason said, using the only makeup buzzword he knew.

Before I could respond, there was a knock at the door. I tossed the iron in the sink and threw myself onto the bed. Jason opened the door to a three-foot-tall Filipina chomping gum and twirling her hair. Eva looked nothing like her photos online. In fact, she kind of resembled one of those little island pygmies from *Gulliver's Travels.*

"Eva?" he exclaimed, trying to mask his discomfort.

"Hi, guys," she purred as she walked over to a chair and sat down.

My mind froze momentarily as my eyes struggled to process the image before me.

"Why is everybody so giggly?" she asked.

Mainly because you didn't mention that you were a garden gnome in your profile, I thought.

Further nervous laughter ensued until finally Jason cut to the chase. "So, should we talk business?"

I took this to mean he was willing to look past the munchkin factor and proceed as planned.

"I'm gonna need three hundred dollars before talking shop," Eva announced, still chomping on her gum. "That covers my bills and my door fee." According to Eva, the kind of "party" we were going to have was entirely up to us. In other words, whatever was going to happen hinged upon how much more cash we were willing to fork over.

I really didn't get why Bilbo Baggins was being such a shady little bastard. But Jason handed over three hundred bucks.

"What can you do for three hundred more?" he asked.

Eva laughed. "Can you hold on for a sec?" We waited patiently while she called her manicurist and pushed her nail appointment back an hour.

"Yeah, there's something going on with the gel," she was saying. "I think it's lifting. Also, the little Swarovski crystal fell off. You said that was gonna stay on. I miss my blingy pinkie!" she whined.

Once she hung up, Jason notified me that he needed to run down to the ATM for more cash. "I'll be right back," he said, darting out of the room with purpose.

Alone with Eva, I was even less comfortable. She sat in her chair, laughing and text-messaging friends. I offered her a drink, which she declined kind of disdainfully, as if I'd proffered a bottle labeled DATE RAPE. (I hadn't thought of it before, but one drug-laden cocktail and I could have easily scored my whole three hundred bucks back.) Once she was done with her texting, she turned to me and, naturally, started telling me about her family.

"My father left when I was very young," she said. (Shocker.) "And my mother raised me all alone."

I felt like I was in an Oliver Stone retelling of *Rumpelstiltskin*. Thankfully, my husband burst back into the room just before she asked me to start spinning the bedsheets into gold.

As soon as the door closed behind him, Eva laid out the game plan.

"Okay, so, I'm gonna go down on him, and you can sit on his face. Cool?"

I was jarred by how fast she got down to business. "Um . . . okay." I gulped.

Just as she started to pull off her rip-away outfit, my husband stopped her. "Wait!" he said. "I couldn't get any more money out!"

"What?" Eva's eyes turned dark. She was a shark and we were her prey.

"I'm already maxed out at the ATM for the day," he explained pathetically.

The shark looked angry.

"Do you accept cashier's checks?" I tried.

"No," she said, putting her top on and getting back on her phone.

"They don't have enough money. Just pull around front. I'm coming down."

I was so embarrassed. Apologizing profusely, I walked Eva out, thanked her for her time, and promised we'd get in touch once we figured out the cash situation. As soon as the door was locked and Eva was gone, I let out a huge cry of frustration.

"Babe! You totally embarrassed me in front of the whore! Now she thinks we can't afford her."

It was getting late, and the surprise party was set to start within the hour. On our way downstairs, I convinced my husband to stay another night in Vegas. My ulterior motive, of course, being *Operation: Find a Whore.* Still reeling from the Hervé Villechaize debacle, I decided to take an alternate approach. I walked up to the youngest concierge I could find and gave it to him straight.

"Dude! I'm having the worst hooker luck! Can you help?"

He looked me in the eye the way drug dealers do when they're trying to assess whether or not you're an undercover cop, then handed me a pamphlet.

Seated in a festive ballroom, waiting to shout "Surprise!",

my husband and I perused pictures of the "merchandise." I felt like one of those super rich guys in *Hostel 2* who murders for sport. The pamphlet gave me hope. *Finally,* I thought. *Real professionals.*

The next day we hung poolside with Gert, Alan, and their boys. At one o'clock, I feigned exhaustion and scurried up to the room, with Jason close behind. This time around, I dressed a bit more casual (no eyeliner). At two on the dot, just as our whore was due to arrive, we heard Gert and Alan's boys running down the hall with their nanny. For a brief moment, I panicked.

"Babe, get those two into their room! The whore is going to be here any minute."

I pressed my face firmly against the peephole to see if I could collect any more data, but the entire frame went dark. *Knock, knock, knock*. Those kids! Without thinking, I flung open the door and reached out to grab the little culprits. Instead of baby swim trunks, however, I got a face full of silicone.

"Hi! I'm Keisha."

It took me a second to process what was going on. Did Gerty and Alan hire a new nanny? Did the boys morph into a giant whore on their walk down the hall? Seeing the shock on my face, my husband stepped in.

Keisha was an Amazonian-looking blonde with tanning-bed skin and extentions down to her ass. She wore a low-cut neon blue dress that expertly showed off her implants, which were securely fastened to opposite sides of her chest. Her stomach was tiny and her limbs were long. She had big blue eyes and wore frosted pink lipstick. She looked like a Barbie come to life, aside from the fact that her tits hated each other.

"Welcome!" Jason said broadly, still in *Fantasy Island* mode.

"Where did the boys go?" I asked.

"Oh, they are so cute!" she said. "They're looking out the window in the hall with their sitter. I rode the elevator up with them."

"You didn't tell them—?" I started, and then revised my question. "They didn't see you come in here, did they?"

"No! I am really discreet. I usually just get away with saying I'm somebody's cousin." She glanced down at her Swarovski-encrusted manicure, apparently the universal symbol of whores everywhere.

The birthday present was going to happen this time, if only because I couldn't stomach another night in Vegas. I pulled myself together and tried to be as clear as possible.

"Seriously, Jason is so hard to shop for. So I want you to go down on him for six hundred bucks."

"Great," she said cheerily. Finally the *Red Shoe Diaries* version of our Vegas weekend was about to commence. "Just so you know, I don't do girls, so any pleasure you get is gonna be from your husband," Keisha cautioned.

I nodded my head, secretly resenting Keisha for not wanting to ravage me. I was in way better shape than Jason, and on top of that, I was waxed like a dolphin.

Slightly less intrigued now, bordering on bored, I listened as Keisha walked us through an extensive list of potential upsets: wife gets hurt and wants to stop; husband can't get erect; wife and husband can't focus because they are too aware of the other's emotions; and so on and so forth.

With sweaty palms, clearly a by-product of all the newly discovered potential for failure, my husband undressed and sat on the bed. Keisha instructed me to do the same. The buxom beauty climbed up on my husband, fastened a condom over his semi-erect penis, and went to work. Instantly, my excitement returned. This was the easiest sex I'd ever had! Happy birthday to everyone!

Jason, however, seemed less thrilled. His body was frozen and his eyes bulged out of his head, locked on me like a math teacher during a Calculus final. I started to worry.

"Do you want to go down on him a bit too?" Keisha suggested.

"Hmm . . . I think you got it covered," I said, opening a bag of Kettle Chips from the minibar and plopping back down beside them.

"Honey, why don't you get involved." Jason said sternly.

Feeling the pressure from both my husband and the woman I imagined was the *only* hooker on the planet who didn't find me irresistible, I obliged. I grabbed my husband's cock with conviction and performed my signature hand job–blow job combo trick for Keisha's benefit. She complimented me on my skills, which almost made me forgive her for not trying to eat my pussy.

"Good job, Jenny! You're really deep-throating that thing!"

"See, baby? I am kind of good at this," I said. Jason's dick went limp in my gloating mouth.

"Stay focused!" Keisha said, smacking me on the head, causing me to choke. Coughing up saliva and potato chip remnants, I sputtered, "Does anyone else kind of feel like Jason's a giant baby and we're putting a weird sex diaper on him?"

"Just you, Jen," Jason said. He sat up and put his underwear back on. The moment had passed.

"Wait, we're done?"

"For now," he sighed.

We spent the next half hour lying in bed with Keisha, listening to stories about her crazy life. She told us about the guy who makes her and a friend come over, call a male prostitute, then order him to suck the male prostitute's dick. Then there was the innocent-looking couple from Washington that wanted Keisha to go home and take a laxative so she could come back later and shit on the husband while the wife took photos.

The thing that struck me the most was how casual and seemingly well-adjusted Keisha was. She was articulate, gregarious, and, were it not for the torpedo boobs, the type of girl who totally *could* be your cousin (if your cousin was a prostitute).

As our time came to a close, Keisha apologized. She told us to call her if we wanted to try again later that evening. We nodded solemnly, and she made one final attempt at lightening the mood by saying, "See, your husband must really love you. He couldn't even stay excited by the idea of another woman."

I smiled and gave her one of those hugs I save for people who I want to make regret not fucking me. With that, we bid her farewell.

On the plane ride home, I texted Keisha to thank her. I secretly hoped she would write back, saying that she regretted not fucking me, but sadly, she didn't. Whatever it was she did do for that six hundred bucks totally worked. For me, anyway. Just sitting next to my husband was somehow more arousing. Even though the actual act was relatively boring and a financial bust, the reliving of it grew hotter and hotter in my mind. When you are in a relationship, it's often easy to lose sight of the fact that other women want to suck your man's dick (even if they're doing it for money). When you witness it with your own eyes, it really helps you appreciate what you have. It's kind of like seeing an old sweater look super cute on one of your girlfriends and realizing you love it again. Not that I'd ever stopped loving my husband; I'd just already owned him for five fashion seasons.

"What a sweet whore," I said, staring down at the flickering lights of Las Vegas.

Jason laughed and grabbed my leg. Something was rekindled between us. Or perhaps something blossomed that had never been there before.

I kissed him passionately, then bashed my forehead against his. "So," I asked, "any idea what you're getting me for *my* birthday?"

7.

Hand Jobs: The Fine Art of Getting a Mani-Pedi Next to Your Husband's Ex (Who Hates You)

So remember when I said that Jason's ex went back into the past? Well, she kind of did for a while. Then, without warning, she was thrust back into my present. I know what you're thinking: I was probably the one to "thrust" her there. But this time it was sheer coincidence and I was merely an innocent—albeit well-manicured—bystander.

Two years had passed, and Baz and I were officially acquaintances who rarely spoke yet held each other in high regard. That was, until I decided it would be a great idea to write a blog post for Playboy.com about the time I hid in my agent Sarah's trunk in order to have a look at her. During our short-lived tryst, I guess I failed to mention any of the previous capers I'd pulled to orchestrate/will our "chance meeting" into existence. I was too caught up in the moment to harp on things of the past. Once Baz and I were together, it was always about the future. Unless, of course, she was telling me stories about dating my husband, in which case, it was about the past. I understand that reading about herself on the Web under a picture of a scary woman drenched in blood wielding a knife with the words OBSESSED EX scrawled underneath was probably a bit of a shock. But the essay was never meant to be hurtful. I came clean about hiding in a trunk to see Baz in an attempt to help other crazy women feel less ashamed for hiding in trunks of their own. I was trying to do something good for humanity, not piss off a girl I spent years trying to woo.

When the article ran, Baz and I were broken up on good terms. Out of respect for Jason, we stayed out of each other's lives, save for the occasional text when either of us had work news or access to a killer sample sale. I assumed she'd read my story the way I naïvely assumed the entire world read my story. Also, because I texted her when it went up. She responded, saying that she would check it out and that she hoped I'd changed her name.

It only occurred to me later that she never followed up with me. I attributed it to her being busy and/or intimidated by my incredible gift for writing, and that she shrugged the whole thing off.

Ten months later, I was forced to infer that Baz *had* read the post. Also that she chose not to write back because she decided she fucking hated me.

Everything I know about developing healthy relationships with other women I learned from my mother, which may be why I thought it was a "fun" idea to write an article about Baz with absolutely no permission whatsoever—like a girly bonding thing. I was wrong. I told my mom as much when she came to L.A. to visit me with her husband, John.

"Mom," I said. "You're the reason I can't have normal relationships with women."

"No, I'm not!" she responded, giggling. "It's because we're

so hot and all other women are jealous." Moms really do know how to put things in perspective.

After years of short-lived romances with weird guys she easily talked into piercing their ear cartilage, my mom finally found a guy she could live with without mentally castrating. She and her husband, John, made it to their eight-year wedding anniversary and drove up from San Diego for the weekend to flaunt their success. As a little midday treat, I thought it'd be fun to take them for mani-pedis. After breakfast, I offered up the plan, praying my mom wasn't going to embarrass me by still being in her weird toe ring phase. John agreed to join but was only willing to get a manicure with "no buffing and absolutely no clear polish."

Around noon, we jumped in my car and drove to my favorite nail spot on Beverly Boulevard, Hand Jobs. It being my favorite nail spot has little to do with how well the girls do nails and more to do with the fact that it's situated next door to the best coffeehouse in the city. The salon owner, a crazy Korean lady named Linda, is a total starfucker who speaks to me only when I'm with Jason. Of course, she doesn't actually call him Jason. Simply, "Amewica Piee!" I once caught her Googling images of him in the waxing room while chanting under her breath, "Amerwica Piee, Amerwica Piee," like she was about to have an orgasm. The store is covered in framed posters of '80s French manicured acrylics holding roses, and the bathroom always has an open Tupperware container half-filled with banana leaves and minced meat sitting near the sink.

The easiest route from my house to the nail salon takes me straight past Baz's apartment. And to be honest, even if it weren't the easiest route, I probably would have driven by anyway, because I had tourists with me and Baz's place was on my "Jenny's Legends of Hollywood" tour. It'd been almost a year since I saw Baz face-to-face, and I hadn't thought much about her in as long a time. (Except for a couple months earlier when I wrote that essay about hiding in a trunk to meet her. And, of course, when I'm taking anyone on my "Jenny's Legends of Hollywood" tour.)

As we drove down the hill at a cool 10 mph, I motioned to my left, pointing out Baz's top-floor unit. My mom rolled down her window, trying to get a better look. Then, almost like the Jaws on the Universal Studios Tour, Baz appeared on the opposite corner, walking her dog.

"Oh my God! That was Baz! Did you just see her?" I craned my neck to get another glimpse.

"I saw her," John said.

"Where? I was looking at the apartment." My mom spun around in her seat like she'd just missed a humpback whale breach.

"Should I go around the block?"

"No," John answered before my mom could say yes.

"You're right. We can't get greedy. That was an amazing sighting, and I have to tell you guys, it rarely happens for first-timers like yourselves. Consider it an anniversary mitzvah."

"It didn't happen for me," my mom pouted.

"I'll buy you an iced coffee," John teased.

As we pulled up to the salon, even from the outside, Hand Jobs looked packed. Linda stood at the entrance and squinted at me like she'd never seen me before in her life.

"Hi, Linda! Remember me? Jenny? Three manicures and two pedicures, please."

Linda pretended not to speak English and motioned for us to sit down. After fifteen minutes, my mom and I were seated in the giant pedicure chairs that Linda was too cheap to fix the massage features on, while John went next door for coffee.

"Two iced coffees, black!" I called out to him, vacillating between two equally cyanotic shades of OPI.

Just as I relaxed into my seat, my phone rang. It was Jason. I was excited to share the news.

"Hey, baby! Guess who we just saw walking her dog on the way here? Baz! Can you believe it?! I told my mom it was like seeing Moby Dick. I honestly haven't seen her in forever! How wild is that? And, baby? She has a short butch haircut again."

Jason was boarding a plane for New York, so he cut me off and told me he'd call when he landed. I told him I loved him, to have a safe flight, and that I couldn't believe he and Baz ever dated.

My mom snuck off to the bathroom, no doubt to remove her toe jewelry before I gave her shit. As she scampered past, I glanced over at the door to see if John was back with the coffees. Standing in his place, however, was someone else. Someone who upon second glance looked a lot like Baz.

"Baaaaz!" Linda cried out, like she was being reunited with her mother, whose visa finally came through.

My mind melted into the hot water soaking my feet, and for a moment I was unable to speak.

It took a few seconds for Baz to notice me, but when she did, I preemptively blurted out a loving hello. Baz looked at me like I was Hitler raping a baby.

She paused before grunting, "Hi."

Linda walked Baz over to the pedicure chair directly across from me, where apparently *her mom* was waiting for her. Baz and her mother were getting pedicures directly across from me and my mother, and I didn't even stalk them to arrange it! I felt like maybe I was being *Punk'd,* but Linda and I both knew I wasn't famous enough for that. This was my karmic payback! And Baz's mom just overheard my entire conversation with Jason about how her daughter looked like a butch.

Now Baz was implying with her gruff hello that we were no longer on good terms. I was shocked she wasn't more excited to see me. Who wouldn't be thrilled to be featured in an essay for Playboy.com? Aside from the omnifarious array of nubile implants belonging to women who aren't old enough to have seen the original *90210,* it is possibly the classiest Web site there is. I felt confused, ashamed, and misunderstood. It was like I was Kelly Taylor in Season Two, made to feel it was her fault for almost getting raped because she wore a sexy costume to a Halloween party. Slightly traumatized, I tucked my face back into my cell phone and pretended to be busy.

When my mom returned, she was still talking about Baz. "Can't believe John saw her and I didn't! If she's such a butch, why do you think Jason dated her for so long?"

I felt all the blood leave my face as I glanced at Baz, busted.

Speechless, I picked up my phone and texted my mom the situation. "You are never going to believe this but in a weird twist of karmic fate, Baz and her mom are sitting in the chairs across from us. The ones with the working massage features!"

My mom looked at me stunned, like Donna Martin's mom when she found out Donna wasn't going to graduate.

"They just put on their shades! I guess they think now we can't see them," my mom wrote back.

I looked up again and noticed that both women were now bedizened in giant black sunglasses that looked like they were from Nordstrom's "Blind People" collection.

"The mom looks like she wants to kill you," my mom wrote.

"Should I say something? Are the glasses a fashion statement or is the mother really blind?"

"I'm not above clocking a blind bitch if I have to," she replied.

John walked back in with our iced coffees.

"Hey, girls! How's it going? Neither of you are getting that fungus-green color, are you?"

I stared at my feet and hoped to god Baz's toes weren't green.

"Her toes are yellow," my mom wrote. "But the color sort of reminds me of baby shit."

"Everybody okay? Did I miss something? You guys didn't drive back by that poor girl's apartment while I was gone, did you?"

My mom whispered something under her breath, which I assume was, "Shut the fuck up, and I'll explain later," because within minutes, John decided he was no longer in the mood for a manicure and went outside for a walk.

Meanwhile, the two seething Lt. Comdr. Geordi La Forges were engaged in furious texting of their own. I racked my brain, trying to remember my essay word for word. Was it perhaps more offensive than I'd thought? Did she somehow misinterpret it as not being slightly tongue-in-cheek? Were there perhaps some other offenses I'd committed that I wasn't even aware of? I didn't understand what could have provoked such anger. The way I saw it, I'd been good to Baz. I secretly took her under my wing after my husband rejected her. I got her extra work on my assistant's short film. (I didn't know in advance that there was going to be nudity.) And I even sent flowers when she finally broke down and got her boobs done (hopefully not for the short film). Why was she being so mean to me?

Since she seemed engrossed in her phone, I thought the easiest way to reach out would be through text. So, from less than five feet away, I took a deep breath and shot her a message.

"Are you mad at me?"

Baz stared up at me like I was Emily Valentine just after she'd doused the West Beverly homecoming float in lighter fluid.

So I did what anyone in my situation would do . . . I sent another text.

"Hike Runyon this week?"

Still nothing.

"Do you have a new boyfriend yet?"

Baz grew angrier by the second and eventually shut her phone off.

Realizing she needed time, I very maturely opted out of my complimentary five-minute neck rub and got up to go. My mom also collected her things before sending me one last text.

"I'm gonna walk past them again so they can see how perky my ass is for my age. Meet you outside?"

I nodded and secretly paid both my tab and Baz's before leaving.

When Baz and her mom didn't call to thank me for the pedis, I realized it was really over. In an attempt to show my own shortcomings as a human, I'd accidentally humiliated her. She had hit her limit. She didn't want to be the Andrea Zuckerman to my Brenda Walsh anymore. She didn't want to *be* anything to me.

From her actions, it was clear that Baz wanted off *The Jenny Show* and I had no choice but to comply. So instead of something degrading and final, like scripting a scene where the character jumps off the Golden Gate Bridge holding the *American Pie* boxed set, I opted for the cleaner, more classic soap opera ending where she simply gets carted off to rehab holding the *American Pie* boxed set. You know, so she can come back for the reunion episode.

8.

Chicks Before Dicks

It took me years to learn how to be friends with girls. And to be honest, I'm still not great at it. Not because I'm one of those whores who's desperate for male attention, but more because I've always feared getting close to one of those whores who's desperate for male attention. You know, the girl who if given the opportunity would fuck your husband right in front of you. And not like, fuck his brains out twenty years from now while your lifeless ashes sit in an urn on the living room mantel, more like accidentally fall on his penis after too much wine in a hot tub while you're asleep (because she drugged you with Benadryl) on a bench next to them. There are just women you can trust and women you can't. As a precaution, I've spent the majority of my life not trusting any of them.

I'm not saying that *all* women will stab you in the back over a man. Some will stab you in the back for other reasons. And to be honest, it's not completely their fault. We live in a society that propagates the notion that a successful woman is hot; has perfect teeth and hair; loves giving blow jobs; drinks beer but doesn't gain weight; has a boyfriend she isn't sick of after two years of him not proposing; looks young enough to still get carded buying cigarettes; dresses like she works for Anna Wintour; and never looks like she's trying as hard as she's actually trying to be motherfucking perfect.

When you put unrealistic expectations on people, they inevitably fall short, start to feel inadequate, and try to fuck your husband. It's just science, people! As a result, the female species is at odds with itself. Every woman is a threat in some way or another because we've bought in to the lie that love and approval are given to only a select few. But those few are never girls you actually know. They are the elusive women of the *Vanity Fair* "Fairground" section. They are the strangers you secretly follow on Instagram. And they are the bitches you hear telling Giuliana Rancic they never break out. This feeling of falling short makes people desperate. And when women are desperate, they get crazy. Again, science!

I'm just as much a competitive psycho cunt as the next girl. As an actress, or actr-ish, I'm jealous of everyone, regardless of gender or age. Sometimes parents will ask me how they go about getting their kids into acting, and my first thought is never, *Oh how cute!* It's always, *Fuck your kid! I will fucking cut your kid! If they think they are just gonna waltz into a business that has bled my soul dry for over a decade and snag an* NCIS: Los Angeles *guest spot out from under me, they are gonna have to pry it out of my cold dead hands! No way! No fucking way!*

As an adult, I've come to terms with the reality of my situation. I'm probably never going to be scouted at the mall. I'm never letting your toddler get in the way of my career, but I'm also never going to have upper thighs that don't touch. Accepting my flaws and feeling less like I need to kill or be killed (except when it comes to your kid) has helped me sustain a handful of decent female relationships. None of which look anything like the unconditional bonds I see women having in TV and film, partly because women aren't that simple, and partly because everyone's love is conditional. The reality is—and I hate to be the bearer of bad news, here—even your best girlfriends can't fucking stand you.

It's not your fault. You just aren't them; ergo, you have issues, issues that could be solved if you just heeded their advice and became exactly like them. Not that they are perfect. They hate themselves too. But trust me, they think they have their shit figured out more than you do at least.

Unlike men, women enjoy analyzing the shit out of something until they're blue in the face. When one of my girlfriends gets up from the table to take a phone call, you better believe the rest of the table is discussing how she should change her life. And most of the time, they're right. Nobody knows what a hot mess you are more than the other hot messes you call friends.

My biggest train wreck of a friend is Simone Chevallier. (She picked this name for the book, which I think says a lot.) Her nickname in college was Captain Blow Job. Simone is five foot eight with brown hair, green eyes, and a rack that could save you in a car accident. She's the type of girl who dates two brothers at once, then doesn't understand why she's in trouble when they find out about each other. She's stolen boyfriends, derailed engagements, and even inspired the occasional divorce. She never has a real boyfriend, but she's always in a fight with some guy over text about why he only calls her after midnight. I don't think Simone means to be such a femme fatale. . . . No, wait, actually I do. She has major daddy issues, is damaged as all fuck, and as a result, is one of the most fun people ever! She has a wicked sense of humor, loves drama, and is always up for an adventure. I met Simone in the sixth grade when my sister and I were shuttled off to live with our father in Arizona. Standing on the scorching hot playground in my J.Crew khakis and inappropriately warm button-up, Simone approached me boldly and said, "You're pretty. I think we should be friends."

She was shallow even then. Simone prizes looks above most things in both women and men. The night before my first date with my husband, Jason, Simone randomly spotted him out at a club.

"Hey, that *American Pie* guy you are supposed to go out with just walked into Le Deux," she texted.

"Is he cute?" I asked.

"In like a Jewish way," she said dismissively.

Now, I know what you're thinking: Why would I be friends with a girl who obviously sounds like the type of whore bag I originally said I'd never get close to? Well, that's simple. Simone is a different strain of whore. Which is to say, she has a specific type. While I only date men who look like rabbis, Simone strictly falls for men hot enough to fuck Herb Ritts. And because I'd never date a guy who looked better in my jeans than I do, I've never really had to worry about Simone trying to sabotage my love life. That was until years later, when Jason and I were happily married and his sister Veronica came out from Jersey for the summer.

Veronica is the baby of the family. She is five feet tall and a quarter of that is hair. She's never been seen without eyeliner and has even been known to apply more before going to bed. Her skin is always covered in bronzer, making her look more yam than human. I once saw her cut a guy off in traffic, then pull up next to him, roll down her window, and call him an asshole. She chain-smokes menthol cigarettes, drinks her coffee with a minimum of seven Equals, and always has an opinion about everything. She's like a mini Joe Pesci in the body of a mini Joe Pesci.

"Are you fucking serious with that one?" she asked one night, while we were in the kitchen preparing for a dinner party.

"What do you mean?" I asked, rummaging through the cupboards for little cocktail umbrellas.

"I mean I wouldn't leave a girl like that alone in a room with my cat's dick!" she said, slamming a shot of tequila straight from the bottle.

I peeked into the room and saw Simone dressed in a cherry red satin romper and sensible Lucite heels talking sports with two dudes she didn't yet realize were the bartenders.

This got me thinking. Maybe I was giving Simone too much credit. How did I know what kind of respect she had for me when I wasn't around? Maybe, after enough carb-ridden margaritas, any cock could become her Fun Dip spoon. I was now officially paranoid.

Later that night, after everyone had gone home, I approached my husband about a possible sting operation. My request was simple: Come on to Simone and see what happens.

"Are you nuts?" Jason asked.

"What? I don't see what the big deal is," I said, my face now covered in green zit medicine.

"Flip the roles. How would you feel if I asked you to come on to one of my friends?"

"Babe, be real. It's already obvious all of your friends would want to be with me if given the opportunity." I applied more medicine to a weird pustule forming next to my nipple.

Disgusted, he stared at me. "Your dad really fucked you up."

"Don't worry. I only want to be with you. You won me,"

I assured him, trying to pop the pustule I'd now determined wasn't a zit but an ingrown hair.

"I wasn't worried." He winced as I broke the skin on the pustule and pulled out a thin dark hair. "In fact, I think you totally missed my point. But whatever."

It was obvious Jason wasn't into my plan and needed some convincing—or rather, some passive-aggressive manipulating of his most deep-seated insecurities.

"You're right. Who am I kidding? Simone would never be attracted to you. She only likes models. You're not her type. Waaay too swarthy . . ."

A beat of silence filled the air. Confident, I said nothing.

"You don't think I could get her?" he finally asked. "I modeled as a child, and before I met you, I used to fuck the hottest chicks!"

"Yeah, chicks who thought you were Jason Schwartzman. That's who I thought you were." I drove the knife deeper.

"That's not true. All women love me because of my adorable personality. I'm irresistible. They expect me to be this dorky guy, but once I start talking, they realize how cool I am and instantly fall in love with me. You did!"

"That's because I only like dorks!" I said, getting into bed beside him.

To a certain extent, he was right. Women have always adored him. One of the many things that bond us is our mutual belief that everyone is in love with us. We both feel we could win over anyone, regardless of age, gender, or race. Even people who don't want to love us. For instance, when someone ignores us, we never take that to mean they don't like us. We just assume they can't deal with the intensity of their feelings and have chosen to back away in order to avoid getting hurt. We are very healthy.

"Trust me, I can get any chick I want, including Simone!" he said, taking the bait.

"Then prove it."

I knew I had him.

The following weekend, we planned a dinner with Veronica, Simone, and two other bitches I was pretend-friends with that summer. My suggested plan was for Jason to pick Simone up for dinner while Veronica and I hid in the backseat. (At this point, I was becoming something of a connoisseur when it came to backseat space, size, and comfort. And I was pleased to learn that my car was the one best suited to spying yet.) If she inquired about why he was alone, he would simply say that Veronica and I took a separate car because we were running late. I knew Simone wouldn't ask questions. It was common knowledge that Veronica took a minimum of five hours to get ready for anything. And Simone doesn't really give a shit about topics that don't somehow circle back to her scoring model dick.

Two blocks before reaching Simone's house, Veronica and I jumped in the backseat of my car and threw jackets over our bodies. Simone was already waiting outside her apartment when we pulled up, dressed in a pleated leather schoolgirl skirt, metal stiletto heels, and a low-cut wife-beater. Jason told her Veronica and I had taken a separate car and, as predicted, Simone got in without further question. We took a turn down an adjacent residential street and slowed down to 5 mph.

Jason started his attack slowly.

"You think I'm ugly, don't you?"

It took everything in me to keep from laughing. Not so

much at the comedy of the situation but more out of nervousness. Whenever I'm uncomfortable, I start to giggle. When I have to fire people, I laugh. When someone dies, I laugh. When someone gets divorced, robbed, or even injured, my first impulse is to laugh. For this, I always come off looking like an insensitive asshole, but the honest-to-god truth is that I just can't deal with seeing other people in pain. And by Jason's tone, I could already tell he didn't plan on half-assing his assignment. Things were about to get severely awkward, and I was already dreading the aftermath. Veronica kicked me to shut up as Jason continued.

"It's cool. I'm obviously not your type. I get it."

"What? No! You're cute!"

Simone shifted uncomfortably in her seat.

Chewing holes in the insides of my cheeks to keep from exploding, I couldn't help but appreciate how talented an actor my husband was. Unlike me, who at thirty-three still looks guilty buying beer at a grocery store, Jason commits to his objective 100 percent. It's like a switch gets flipped inside him, and he literally becomes that other person he's portraying. Before I could start beating myself up for being the Jimmy Fallon of our at-home *Saturday Night Live* troupe, Jason switched gears.

"Can you keep a secret?"

"Yeaaah," Simone said, rolling down her window for some air.

"Why don't you give me a blow job," he said, completely cavalier.

Not getting it, Simone tilted her head to the side and looked at him the way your dog looks at you when you're about to leave the house without him.

"I don't get it. You said you were gonna tell me a secret," she said.

"That was the secret. As in, blow me and we won't tell anyone, get it?"

Jason was growing frustrated with Simone the way he does with all his female co-stars. I could already hear his bitching in my head: "She wasn't picking up her cues fast enough, she was talking over my lines, she wasn't listening and reacting. . . ."

Simone started breathing heavily, like she was going to have a panic attack. Guilt-ridden, Veronica nudged me to reveal myself. Turning onto La Cienega, Jason continued to badger Simone.

"Show me one of your tits, and I'll just masturbate on it really quick."

The light turned red and the car sat momentarily idle. My husband and Captain Blow Job were at an impasse, both literally and figuratively.

Veronica and I sat up silently. Simone didn't notice us, because her head was buried in her purse, most likely looking for Mace. Then, taking what must have felt like her only chance at escape, Simone flung open her car door just as Jason hit the gas. The car jerked into first gear and Simone, gripping the door, flew out of the vehicle. Her hands clung tightly to the handle as her metal stilettos dragged behind her, picking up speed. Sparks flew like she was wearing rocket-powered roller skates, and her skirt was pulled up, revealing her bare ass.

"Where is her underwear?" Veronica asked, alarmed.

"Hold on, Simone!" I said.

I climbed into the front seat and tried to secure the door from slamming shut on her fingers.

"Stop the car, you bitch!" Simone cried.

"Baby! Stop the car!"

"I can't just stop, Jen!"

If Jason hit his brakes, Simone might lose her grip and slip under the wheels; if he kept going, she might lose her grip and slip under the wheels. The only option was to gradually coast to a stop and hope Simone's Tracy Anderson DVDs had done their job in strengthening her core.

Simone's arms seemed to be giving out as Jason swerved out of traffic and pulled into a nearby parking lot.

"I'm too cute to die!" she screamed.

As we came to a gradual stop, Simone went rolling. Her heels were fucked up beyond recognition, distracting her from the gravitas of what almost happened to the rest of her.

"These were four hundred dollars, you cunt!"

I stared down at her scalding-hot pumps that were now kitten wedges.

"You risked your life for our friendship! You were willing to throw yourself from a car to avoid fucking my husband!" I said, helping her into the backseat in what I thought would be our total chicks-before-dicks moment.

"Actually, I just don't find Jason hot."

Simone peeked under her skirt to make sure her vagina was still intact.

"You all saw my vagina, didn't you?" she asked, smirking proudly.

After appraising the state of her hair and makeup, Simone demanded we take her to Cedars emergency room for a full-body scan.

Veronica called the other girls waiting for us at the restaurant and tried to explain what happened, but I think all they really got was that Jason asked Simone for a blow job and she tried to kill herself.

Simone lasted only five minutes in the waiting room before setting her sights on a DJ with a broken hand who looked like the type of guy who invites you back to his dorm to listen to house music and then rapes you.

"Have you ever realized that you are kind of that self-serving asshole that you tell your girlfriends not to date?" Veronica said to me, stuffing her face with SunChips from a nearby vending machine.

It was true! More than liking pretty faces, Simone liked people who undervalued her, and I had accidentally done just that. Simone wasn't after my husband. She was probably in my life because she was addicted to my abuse!

"I am so sorry," I said, grabbing her by the arms and sobbing like she had cancer.

She seemed unfazed and assured me payback would be a bitch as she followed the DJ outside for a cigarette and never returned. We waited for a good fifty minutes before realizing we'd been ditched.

Simone called me the next day to sit on the phone with her as she tiptoed out of the DJ's apartment. I tried again to apologize for my behavior, but she wasn't really listening.

"I don't think he has a girlfriend. I searched his place and couldn't find a single rubber band. He's moving out of town in a few weeks because he's taking a job for the government. Do you think I'll hear from him?" she asked with zero irony.

"Of course," I said, knowing she probably wouldn't.

Hanging up, I asked myself why I tried to tempt Simone, one of my oldest friends, with the offer of giving my husband a hummer in West Hollywood traffic. Why would I want to throw a twenty-year friendship under the wheels of a slow-moving SUV? Like most good things in my life, I'd convinced myself that somehow, somewhere, Simone would pull the rug out from under me, as all women were genetically programmed to do. Mistrusting her was unwarranted, unfair, and obviously a product of my own insecurity. The truth was, Simone was more prey than predator, and entirely too self-involved to be intentionally malicious. Her problem was her taste in people. She wasn't out to destroy me. If anything, she was out to destroy herself. I contemplated whether or not Jason could have gotten something out of her had he taken the douche bag "I'm gonna make you feel like shit" approach. But I stopped myself. It didn't matter. I was married to a good guy, and Simone hates good people. That's why she's friends with me.

9.

"You Aren't My Real Father"

Those were the final words of the toast/slam-poem/hate-haiku that my father's new ten-year-old stepson delivered to an engagement party of 150 people. Sandwiched between my dad's haidresser and the lady who stuffed my late grandmother's shih tzu, my husband and I tried to stay calm. As the microphone made its way closer, I had a frightening realization: If I was going to keep my sanity through my dad's wedding weekend, I needed to be on drugs.

After a twelve-year stint of bachelorhood, my father was finally ready to give marriage the fourth old college try. In my unhumble opinion (which is really the only opinion you need to worry about), he had two reasons for doing this: (1) my sister and I just got married and he was copying us, and (2) fear.

At sixty-eight years old, my father knew the day was coming when he'd no longer be able to care for himself. Eventually, he'd lose all mental awareness and I'd gain power of attorney and force him to live in my guesthouse with my mother, his estranged wife. From there, there's really no telling what might happen. I could, perchance, see myself forcing them into giving me the childhood I always wanted. I might hypothetically build a stage in the living room, where I'd perform *Gypsy* every night (with matinees on Wednesdays, Saturdays, and Sundays).

Maybe I'd make them time me holding my breath in the pool. And if I were feeling particularly kinky, I'd even allow them to tuck Jason and me into bed with a story. (Preferably not the one of their divorce. Too many dead babies.)

The third reason for him getting married again also had to do with being in love, but as an outsider, it still felt more like 1 with a subconscious hint of 2.

My dad met Kristen shortly before I met Jason, at one of three bars he used to troll for pussy—specifically, pussy that wasn't friends with other pussy he'd already bedded and stopped calling. Unlike her predecessors, Kristen had a U.S. passport, was over twenty-one, could read, and already owned her own pair of boobs. She didn't need anything from my father, making it a total mystery as to why she'd want to hang out with him. My dad proposed to Kristen just before Jason asked for my hand, and by the time my wedding rolled around, he was already over it and broke up with her. He still brought her to our Napa nuptials as his date, however, because he's a dick like that.

Around Christmas, Kristen wised up and started seeing someone else. And my dad pretended to be unfazed, aside from when he'd call me every morning to play the game "Kristen's Still In Love With Me, Right?" I like my dad best when he's on the verge of an emotional breakdown because that's the only time he actually listens to me—because I'm talking about him.

After one whiny phone call about how he was going to be spending Christmas Eve alone (even though he's Jewish and the holiday means absolutely nothing to him), my guilt kicked in and I invited him out to LA to celebrate with Jason and me.

"You invited your dad out to spend our first Christmas as a married couple with us?" Jason asked, more than a little annoyed. "It's like, I kind of knew before marrying you that you were already married to your father, but I just assumed once we were married that your thing with him would sort of die off." He marched upstairs and slammed the bedroom door, just like my father would.

My enmeshment with my dad did have a tendency to appear to outsiders like we were in a relationship. Especially when I turned twenty and for vanity reasons he started introducing me to people as his "friend" and sleeping in my bed whenever he came to visit me at college. To clarify, I was living in a studio apartment that he was paying for, so in a way I think he actually considered it his bed. And for the record, nothing inappropriate ever happened between us. As long as you consider kissing on the lips appropriate.

"I'm inviting Larry over as a buffer, so deal with it!" Jason called down ten seconds later.

Larry was Jason's best friend. If he were a pageant girl, he'd be Miss Congeniality. He's the guy who no matter where you are in the world knows somebody who owes him a favor. Larry and Jason met in Los Angeles ten years earlier at one of Larry's epic house parties in the Hills. They didn't speak until the next morning, however, when Larry discovered Jason pants-less, covered in Bugles, and passed out on one of his Kingsley-Bate lawn chairs. He was the best man at our wedding and had recently called off his own engagement to a somewhat quirky woman who once, out of anger, shaved a swastika into his dog while he was in Dubai on business.

Around 5 P.M. on a Friday, I picked my dad up from the airport—because he doesn't like that cabs cost money—and brought him back to our house. When we arrived, Larry and Jason were building a fire and drinking scotch. Since he was not a fan of sharing my attention with people, places, or things,

I was certain my dad would make some sort of passive-aggressive comment about why the fuck Larry was over. But as it turned out, my dad was psyched Larry was there. Larry was Jewish, always impeccably dressed, business-minded, newly single, and thirty-five, the same age my dad was in his head. From the minute my dad sat down on the small sliver of couch separating Jason and Larry (even though there was a whole living room filled with empty seats), he didn't stop talking. And everything out of his mouth was in weird single guy code. I only know this because each sentence started with the phrase, "This is single guy code."

An hour and a half after I told her dinner was being served, my sister, Amanda, showed up. Amanda is sixteen months younger than me, and my only full sibling. Before I started dyeing my hair brunette to gain respect from society, people often mistook us for twins. The only real difference is that she is a total bitch and I'm not. Amanda was the kid who, after receiving a subpar haircut at our neighborhood mall, threw herself prostrate on the ground, screaming until my mom dragged her writhing body out to the car and shut her up by promising to buy her a Missoni do-rag. When we started getting allowance, I spent mine on Asian masks, which I used to pretend I was the family's foreign exchange student, and she'd buy long Lee Press-On Nails to pretend she was my wealthy white slave-owner.

Amanda and my father have a completely different relationship than he and I do, in that Amanda doesn't give a fuck what he thinks and as a result my dad ignores her. When my mom decided parenthood wasn't for her, Amanda and I were both deported to Phoenix for a year of living under his roof with his third wife, Ursula. (I named her after the sea witch from *The Little Mermaid* if that gives you any indication of my feelings about her.) After six months, Amanda cracked and begged my mom to take her back. She had little tolerance for my dad's totalitarianism and missed my mom's democratic approach to parenthood, one of the highlights being the *No drinking hard alcohol on school nights* suggestion taped to the fridge. I, meanwhile, found myself staying another four years because I didn't know how to tell him no. I'd been recruited to fill him emotionally and I was too weak and desperate for parental attachment to refuse. Though conditional, he gave me the love and attention my mom saved for her boyfriends. I was devastated to lose Amanda and assumed she felt the same until a girl on the playground at school told me she heard Amanda raving about how excited she was to become an only child.

Just before the beginning of my junior year, and right around the time Ursula sponge-painted every wall in our house period-blood red, my dad told me he was getting a divorce. Besides finding out from him that I got into UCLA because he opened my acceptance envelope without me, this was the best news I'd ever heard come out of his mouth. What I didn't realize at the time was that with both my sister and Ursula gone, I would become my father's only significant other.

At Christmas dinner, my dad had Larry cornered. "I'm in amazing shape, I have all the money I could ever spend, and I'm a local celebrity. I should be thrilled with my life. And I am. I'm so happy," he assured Larry, the only person in the room who was still listening to him. "Kristen and I want different things. It just didn't make sense, so I had to cut her loose, you know? The guy she's dating now, I can tell you right now, that's *all kinds of wrong*. She'll probably never be over me fully. Frankly, I'm surprised she hasn't reached out to wish me a Merry

Christmas." He looked at his phone like one of my desperate girlfriends waiting for a call from a guy who obviously hates her.

"It sounds like you've made up your mind," Larry said, kicking back in his chair and picking his teeth. The rest of us made a mass exodus to the kitchen.

"You get that your dad was totally broken up with, right?" Jason said, loading the dishwasher.

"I know. I almost feel bad for secretly kind of loving it." I smiled.

"Jenny, this is a guy who takes a woman to Paris, then comes home with two albums' worth of pictures of just himself. I'm happy about it too. Good for her! He was leading her on!" Jason offered Kristen a supportive "you go girl" nod—wherever she was.

"I'm completely invisible to him. I don't even know why I came over. If I made more money, maybe he'd give me some respect," my sister said, storming in and scouring the pantry for something sweet.

"I don't think that's true. He gives me respect and I don't make any money," I said, thinking I was helping.

"Hey, now that Kristen has obviously ditched his ass, maybe you guys can get back together," she retaliated.

Jason looked at me sharply. "Don't even think about it, I'm your only man now."

"Sidebar," Amanda said, reappearing with a mouth full of Red Vines, "Do you guys get the vibe that he kind of likes me?"

"Who, Dad?" I asked.

"No," Jason and I answered in unison.

"Not Dad, assholes. Larry." Amanda threw a vine at Jason's head.

Jason and I looked at each other. Were we really that blind?

Were we too busy enjoying the fact that my dad had been dumped to catch Larry crushing on Amanda? The three of us proceeded back into the dining room with caution. Larry immediately noticed Amanda and stopped picking his teeth.

"Check out this picture of me at the top of the Eiffel Tower," my dad said, handing Larry his phone and standing up to use the restroom. "Remember—if it rings, don't answer it. We're sending Kristen to voice mail." He winked conspiratorially.

"Hey, guys," Amanda said, flirty.

My dad ignored Amanda but handed me his empty glass and said "Water" before disappearing out of sight.

When Jason and I looked up, Amanda and Larry were smirking at us. They glanced at each other, then again at us, and started laughing that annoying laugh that people have when they aren't yet in a relationship and still feel superior.

In that moment I knew: Amanda was going to fuck Larry.

When Sunday rolled around, both Amanda and Larry stopped answering their phones. Kristen never called my dad, and he continued to rattle off excuses as to why she didn't for the entire ride to the airport.

Fifteen minutes after we peeled my dad out of our backseat, assuring him that Kristen's new boyfriend was impotent, Amanda returned my call from two days prior.

"So you may wanna sit down for this," she started.

"Okay."

"Well, I'm with Larry. And, well, we're in love."

Both my jaw and the phone fell to the floor. Sure, I thought she'd sleep with Larry. But love? Amanda? The only time I'd heard my sister use the term "love" was when she was talking about that Cartier bracelet you screw on your wrist.

Jason picked up the phone and Amanda explained how instead of going home after Christmas dinner, she and Larry drove up to Santa Barbara and checked into Bacara for the rest of the weekend. Now they had matching tattoos and were considering moving in together.

Jason hung up and stared at me in disbelief.

"My best friend is in love with a bitch, and now I'm gonna be stuck hanging out with her forever!"

"Okay, slow down. . . . She's my *sister*—you were already stuck hanging out with her forever."

"So you're not denying that she's a bitch?"

"No. But she's like a fun bitch."

"What's a fun bitch?"

"It's like someone who's bitchy but still kind of—," I started before he cut me off.

"Just tell me it's not gonna last."

"Relax, it's not gonna last. Amanda is an ice queen. And Larry is a good person. You are working yourself up over nothing."

Six months later, Amanda and Larry were engaged. And despite our initial trepidation, the union proved to be extremely convenient. Whenever we had family obligations, Larry was forced to join. Whenever I was pressured into attending random peripheral friend events, my sister was roped into going as well. Our alliance also gave us the manpower to say no to invitations we might otherwise feel inclined to accept. One particular invitation however, left little room for escape.

Just as Amanda's bridal shower was winding down, my father stood up, ostensibly to toast my sister. (Yes, he insisted on attending the bridal shower. Yes, he was the only guy there. And yes, people gave her lingerie that she was forced to open in front of him.)

"Well, I broke down and gave Kristen the ring back." He chuckled, then looked around the room, awaiting applause.

"That's great news," I said, when what I really felt like saying was, *Why the fuck are you here? This is a bridal shower.*

Later that night over dinner, Jason said to my dad, "I thought Kristen stopped talking to you."

"Nah, she was just playing hard to get. I knew she'd come around, you should see the ring," he said smugly.

"We have. It's the same ring she was wearing nine months ago, right?" Amanda said, annoyed.

My sister's wedding was planned for October 24, so my dad decided November 24 would give us plenty of time to regroup and prepare for his wedding.

"I'm sorry, did you say you are having a wedding? As in, a full-blown, white-dress, toss-the-bouquet wedding?" I asked.

"This is Kristen's first marriage," my father explained. "I can't take that away from her."

"I still don't get how she started talking to you again . . . ," Jason said, perplexed.

"Who's doing your catering? We wanna do the whole mini burgers and shakes thing. Have you seen those?" he asked my sister, who was now an 11 on the 1 to "rip somebody's heart out and eat it" scale.

My dad was literally jacking my sister's big day, and there was nothing anyone could do to stop him. Our mom's marriages, though numerous, were always low-key elopements. Before this, if I got an invite to someone's fourth wedding, I'd probably assume it was a joke and send back a picture of Jason's balls. My dad, unfortunately, wasn't joking, nor did he have any shame in registering for a bunch of redundant kitchen shit at William-Sonoma.

On November 23, my husband and I, along with the newly married Amanda and Larry, boarded a Southwest flight to Phoenix. We got wasted on the plane, and by the time the flight landed, only two of us were in any condition to hail a cab. I was not one of those two.

The cab dropped us off at Kristen's sister's house, where the rehearsal dinner was already in full swing. The place was a mix of second-tier family friends and extras I think he hired for his last wedding. A magician showed up, guessing everyone's birthday. And at one point, I even thought I saw a belly dancer, but it just turned out to be one of Kristen's weird aunts from Israel.

While Amanda and Larry buried themselves in the buffet, I buried myself in Jason's coat pocket, looking for Xanax. Unfortunately, all I found was a Ricola.

"A Ricola? How is this gonna help? I'm off Zoloft and I need soothing!"

I was always going on and off Zoloft. I initially started meds to counter my eating disorder and then stayed on them to deal with the general depression that comes with being an actress married to her father. Over the years, I've vacillated over whether or not I actually need it, and at this particular time I didn't think I did. I was wrong.

"Jason, I'm serious. This whole environment is giving me posttraumatic stress."

When Amanda and Larry resurfaced, they too had reached their breaking point.

"Uncle Ernie just pulled me aside and said, 'You look good. I remember when you were poor,'" Amanda whispered loudly.

"We have an Uncle Ernie?" I asked.

"Aren't you still poor?" Jason continued.

We were angry, hungover, and in need of reprieve. The four of us were staying at my dad's, so even if we left the party, it was only going to be to go back to his house, a place where even bad photos of him still found their way into frames. There was no escaping physically, so we had to do so emotionally.

"Do you think your new stepbrother has weed?" Jason asked, dead serious.

"He's ten. Maybe? I don't know. What age do kids start dealing drugs these days?"

In L.A., you can buy marijuana as easy as you can a bottle of milk. In Arizona, I think you go to jail for just being Mexican. We couldn't risk involving my stepbrother—not because we thought it was immoral to corrupt a child, but rather because we thought he looked like a narc.

"You're the only one of us who went to high school here," Amanda said. "Can't you make some calls?"

"I haven't lived here in over thirteen years. And even when I did, the only drug I had access to was Advil Cold and Sinus."

"It's true, you guys, Jenny wasn't cool. I've seen her yearbook. She wore suspenders. I say we go with the ten-year-old." Jason was pacing anxiously.

This was all the motivation I needed. I couldn't let Jason know he was right about my cool status. The fact that my dad completely pirated my teens was a source of shame. The years I should have spent buying drugs with friends were instead spent riding on the back of a tandem bicycle listening to a fifty-year-old man talk about "the market." I didn't have time to misbehave because I was too consumed with trying to anticipate his every want and need. I wanted him to love me, to see me, and was willing to do just about anything to make that happen. Sophomore year, I let his barber attempt the "Jennifer Aniston," leaving me instead with the "Kato Kaelin." Junior year, I acquiesced and let him get me a personalized license plate that read: STR8AS. These were all things I needed to keep buried in the past. I was going to find weed even if it meant selling my new ten-year-old stepbrother to a Mexican cartel.

I snuck outside and texted the only person I could think of who might be able to help, my friend Sky. Sky still owed me from hooking her up with the fake ID my mom scored me in Mexico. And though she moved away years ago, I knew she was still Facebook friends with the crowd that made their own acid and had babies at sixteen. Holding my breath, I sent her a text message.

"Where is there grass in Phoenix?"

"U R A DORK," she wrote back promptly.

Oh my God, I'm in my hometown for less than twenty-four hours, and already I've been reminded of how uncool I was—twice. Riddled with anxiety, I pulled on my hair to make sure my locks weren't shriveling back up into "the Rachel."

Sky then responded with a number and a name: "Joe."

Feeling like I'd just received the coordinates to One-Eyed Willie's hidden treasure ship, I rushed back inside.

"Guys, guys, I totally got a number!"

"Let me see," Jason said as he snatched my phone away. "She did."

"Thanks for fucking confirming." I took the phone back. "Wait, you have to make the call. I'm really awkward with drug dealers." I hoped that didn't imply that I'd never actually met a drug dealer.

"I'll do it," Larry said, taking the phone from both of us.

Larry ducked outside to make the call. While he was gone, my dad zeroed in on us from across the room.

"This is pretty great, right?" he said, nodding in agreement as if someone else had just asked the question.

"Totally," Jason agreed.

Just as Amanda started talking, my dad produced a car

key and stared into Jason's eyes with the urgency of twenty-four-hour palm reader.

"Ever drive a Ferrari?" he asked, tipsy.

"I ha—," Amanda started before being cut off yet again.

"I'll let you guys drive this home if you promise to be careful," he said, pretending to be generous but really just looking for someone to drive his car back to the house for him.

Jason couldn't give a fuck about a Ferrari. The only thing any of us cared about was being in a vehicle with an engine that could transport our bodies to a place where giant buds of marijuana would be rolled up, set on fire, and placed delicately in our mouths. We would have driven a Fred Flintstone convertible that could only be operated by barefoot running if it meant getting stoned.

The party was winding down, and my dad suggested we get a head start back to his place. In other words, he was already growing impatient that his car wasn't safely back in its garage.

Larry returned, and the four of us rushed out like we'd just finished cheating on the PSATs. Once both doors were shut and my sister and I were folded into the trunk/backseat, Larry confirmed our wildest hopes.

"His name is Joe and we are getting pot!"

"Thank God," Jason said, peeling out of the driveway and over a curb.

Joe lived minutes from Kristen's sister's place, and I was familiar enough with the street names to start shouting out directions. We took down the top so my sister and I could feel our necks again and blasted the only CD in my dad's car since 1982, the *Rocky III* soundtrack. After about twenty minutes of harmonizing on "Eye of the Tiger," Jason slowed down.

"Jenny, you clearly don't know where the fuck you're going, because now we're back in front of Kristen's sister's house."

Shit. We totally were. I reminded everyone I hadn't lived there in thirteen years while Larry punched Joe's address into his iPhone. After following the GPS ten miles in the opposite direction, we arrived at our destination.

Taking in the scene, I started to panic. Joe's house wasn't some stucco, cookie-cutter housing development erected during the mid-'90s real estate boom. It was a palatial, newly remodeled spec house at the top of Camelback Mountain. Joe was obviously a kingpin.

Dubious, Larry checked the address again. "This is it," he confirmed.

Jason turned off the car, and the four of us sat silently in the driveway. The landscape lights were off, and we couldn't make out any activity coming from inside the home.

"This looks like the type of place where I could get shot with a machine gun," I whispered.

"We'll all go in together, get the weed, and be back in the car in under five minutes," Jason said to himself.

The guys pried us out of the backseat like paramedics, and we made our way up the tall staircase to the front entrance. When we got there, Larry pressed the buzzer.

A friendly voice responded without even asking who we were. "Yo, come on in. I'm just getting out of the pool."

"This guy's drug-dealing skills need work. He didn't even ask us for a password," I said.

Nobody responded.

The entrance opened up to a large outdoor terrace. We proceeded back past a pool surrounded by looming palm trees and nouveau riche Italian marble. To the right, a sliding glass door was open, and the same voice called out to us from inside.

"Over here!"

We walked inside to find Joe, a chubby, white, Jewish kid lounging on a giant leather couch in a chenille bathrobe.

"Hey, guys, I ordered the fight. What can I get you to drink?"

Though I appreciated his hospitality and was happy to see he wasn't polishing a gun or doing coke off a machete, I was still unsettled about hanging out in his *Scarface* lair.

"I think we just wanted to grab some pot," I said uneasily.

Finally out of patience with what a total amateur I was, Amanda pulled me aside. "Jenny, you have to smoke a bowl with your dealer and pretend you're his friend before you just bail with his weed like an asshole, okay?"

Unfazed, Joe walked over to his fridge and pulled out three bags of giant green buds. "What kind of high you guys looking for?"

"I don't know, just something that could take the edge off seeing my dad slow-dance to 'Unchained Melody' in the next twenty-four hours," I said.

Joe weighed out enough pot to last us through my dad's fifth and sixth weddings, and just to be safe, we bought all of it.

The five of us smoked, and within minutes Joe's house seemed like the safest place on earth.

I kicked off my shoes and relaxed into a small motorized car parked in the hallway.

While Jason and Larry got sucked into the boxing match, Joe took Amanda and me on a tour.

The place was huge but primarily empty. The light fixtures were nowhere to be seen, closet doors were missing, and even the stove was pulled out. Joe explained that the house wasn't actually his. He was just a squatter, staying there until his friend, an investor, got his money out of the place. Due to the housing crisis, the property had sat dormant on the market for just over two years before the contractor started selling off bits and pieces to make the mortgage.

Five or six rides in the elevator that only covered three floors later, Joe excused himself to the restroom. When he reappeared, he was dressed as a giant pink bunny.

I knew I was stoned. But not *that* stoned.

"Did we take acid?" I asked earnestly, trying to throw my minicar into reverse.

Wide-eyed, Amanda approached Joe slowly like he was E.T. and started petting his face.

"It's cool! He's real!" she exclaimed through bloodshot eyes.

The bunny suit was left over from Halloween, and Joe thought we might want to take some pictures of him in it.

"Um . . . Yes, please!" Jason said, now standing in the hallway, eating a giant bowl of Oreos drenched in milk with a spoon.

Abandoning my mini vehicle in the elevator, I escorted Joe outside for a photo shoot.

Larry and Jason hoisted him onto the hood of the Ferrari, and Amanda started snapping shots. Next, we positioned him under the front wheel as if he were roadkill.

"Does anyone have any fake blood?" Jason asked.

"Just put some Oreo juice on him!" Amanda suggested.

Jason drizzled milk over Joe's chest as he made a valiant attempt to be America's Next Top Model. And for a few brief minutes that seemed like a stoner's hour, I started to get a sense of what a normal adolescence felt like.

Suddenly, the car phone started ringing. It was my dad.

Looking at my watch, I noticed it was now two in the morning. We'd been with Joe for over four hours.

"Who still has a car phone?" Joe asked.

"The guy who still listens to the *Rocky III* soundtrack on disc," Larry explained.

"We have to go! We are gonna be in so much trouble, and we can't take Joe with us! Joe get away from the car!" I sounded like a paranoid nineteen-year-old waiting for the results to an HPV test.

"Everyone shut up," Jason said, helping Joe up and nibbling an Oreo crumb off his chest. "Joe, look, dude, we've given you four hours of our lives for an ounce of weed. We gotta get home."

"That's only an ounce?" I asked.

"An ounce is a lot," everyone said in unison.

"*Fine! I was a dork in high school.* This is the first time I've had fun, okay?"

"She and my dad were married, she didn't get out much. I lived with my mom. I totally know what an ounce looks like." Amanda fixed Joe's ears and kissed him on the cheek.

We bade Joe farewell and drove home.

"It's two A.M. He's getting married in less than eight hours. Why is he still awake?" I rambled as we pulled through the security gate of my dad's house.

"Maybe it was a pocket dial," Larry offered reassuringly.

The house lights were out and everything seemed quiet. With a renewed sense of victory, we pressed the garage door opener to go inside. There, standing exactly five feet eight in slippers (with lifts) was my dad. He was wide awake.

"Hey! Where have you guys been?" he said. He was completely sober now.

Reeking of marijuana, none of us had an answer. I started to make up some ridiculous story about taking Jason to see my old high school but got distracted by a framed photo of my dad holding another framed photo of my dad. Amanda walked straight past us and went to the fridge to make a sandwich.

All my dad seemed to want to talk about was the Ferrari, so it fell on Jason and Larry to indulge him. I just stood there nodding until eventually, Larry's true understanding of something my dad actually knew very little about put him to sleep.

The four of us snuck upstairs to my high school bedroom and passed around the first joint ever to arrive on the premises. Kristen's son slept soundly in the room next door, and on more than one occasion we were tempted to wake him and ask if he wanted a toke. We decided against it because we figured he was too young. Also because in time, he would have to learn that finding weed isn't always easy. Kids need to work for things in order to appreciate them. Jason was the first one to say out loud what I think all of us were thinking.

"I am so glad you guys are stuck dealing with this shit too. This would really suck if I were here alone."

We all smiled. None of us could respond. We were also way too stoned to know how to use words.

The next day, my father married Kristen in an over-the-top ceremony on a golf course. The four of us were late because Amanda wasn't happy with her updo. But we managed to sneak in just in time to see my dad ride up to the chuppah on horseback. Kristen was carried down the aisle on the backs of five topless dudes I recognized from the summer I worked at Bobby McGee's, and her ten-year-old trailed behind her, doing the Running Man. The sense of impending doom I'd felt the night before seemed to dissolve in the daylight. Everyone was optimistic and blown away by the mini burgers. Kristen looked gorgeous and in love and not at all concerned with the fact that she'd just married a sixty-eight-year-old man who drinks his coffee through a straw and wears G-string underwear.

For me, the day signified the end of an era. I was no longer my father's spouse. I was my own woman, with my own husband and my own ounce of weed.

After the cake was served, the mic made its way yet again toward our table. This time, however, I took it. And with a sense of relief, I said:

"Raise your hand if you wanna get high!"

10.

One Shade of Grey

Marriage is amazing. It's like living with your best friend—someone you sleep with, laugh with, cry with, and eventually turn into the Crypt Keeper right in front of like it's no big deal. But you know what's hotter than having sex with your best friend for all of eternity?

Everything.

The truth is, people are perfect only when you don't know them. I once dated a guy who in retrospect may have been a mannequin, and I still managed to base my happiness solely upon his approval for a solid three months. When you're sleeping with a stranger, you aren't really vulnerable, even though you think you are when you're filling your iPod with songs you've secretly dedicated to them and writing in your journal about how you wish they really knew you. But alas, if they knew you, the fantasy would be over and you would be sleeping with a real person, which is, as I stated earlier, infinitely more complicated than fucking a mannequin.

Most of us can only hope to find that perfect person who accepts us for all that we are and all that we aren't. Richard Bach wrote, "A soulmate is someone who has locks that fit our keys and keys to fit our locks." For Jason and me, it was more like he didn't even try the lock. He just wrapped a big rock in some annoying Urban Outfitters T-shirt I never would have approved of and chucked it haphazardly through my bathroom window while I was picking a chin zit. But once he was in, *he was in*!

I wouldn't classify our first meeting as love at first sight—unless I was speaking for him, which I have no problem doing. So yes, let's go with, it was love at first sight (for him). As for me, I was a little taken aback by the fact that five minutes into our introduction, he excused himself to the restroom by saying, "I'm gonna go do some coke in the bathroom. Oh, and also, I hate black people." When he returned, it was clear he was joking about the coke. We spent the rest of the night bonding over our Zoloft prescriptions and insane parents. Finding out someone is the same kind of crazy that you are is a special kind of turn-on. We didn't sleep together until a week or two later, and when we did I think I made him bleed from how intensely I was clawing my way into his flesh. You know, the way you do when you really want someone to understand you. Our chemistry was electric, and even holding hands made my heart feel like it was going to beat straight out of my chest. But, like all relationships, ours matured into something more stable. And eventually, squeezing the pus out of his closed-up earring holes replaced sex as my favorite thing to do before bed.

Don't get me wrong, my desire for my husband hasn't weakened, just my own motivation to do anything about it. It's kind of like the treadmill: awesome and rewarding once it's over, but after a bowl of pasta, two Skinny Cow ice cream bars, and a Gilt Groupe flash sale, just sort of hard to jump into.

For many women (the ones who aren't liars), it's work to stay sexually stimulated by a partner who's returning our phone calls and not mindfucking us into believing that we're ever so slightly inadequate. In a healthy marriage there is stability, security, and individual packs of Pirate's Booty. Sex is always an option—but so is getting stoned and watching *Mad Men.* Like anything that is available freely and constantly, there's just no real urgency about it. Especially when *Mad Men* is on.

That was, until me and 65 million other women met Christian Grey.

Fifty Shades of Grey by E. L. James crept into my life kind of the same way my husband did: while I was preoccupied with a chin zit.

I don't typically read books that appeal to women who saw *The Notebook,* wear things from the Victoria's Secret PINK collection, or happen to be my mother-in-law. I like depressed German authors who write stories about people whose lives start out bad and then get worse. The most pop I've ever delved into was that whole *Dragon Tattoo* book, and even then, I had to chew off the cover for fear that people in book clubs would start trying to recruit me.

I was browsing through a bookstore in Santa Monica, unconsciously peeling a layer of skin off an underground whitehead, when a salesgirl asked if I'd read the *Fifty Shades of Grey* trilogy.

"Really?" I said, more than a little disturbed. Was it the fresh blood gushing out of my face? My new bangs? The fact that the bottom half of my body was covered in peanut brittle? "Do I look like someone who's read any trilogy ever?"

"Trust me, this isn't your typical trilogy." She handed me the first book with a look of confidence I'd seen only on the lady who does my filler. "It will change your sex life in a week."

To be honest, I wasn't necessarily convinced my sex life needed changing. I was over flying to Vegas and looking for hired help. I was perfectly okay with our dogs watching Jason try to get an erection, and equally fine with them sitting on my face while he was going down on me. (Just to clarify: We don't fuck dogs. I just get distracted during sex and sometimes I talk to my dogs and braid their hair when Jason's going down on me.)

It's not that I'm not by nature a sexual person. It's just that I'm never good at anything when I know I have to be serious. Sex with your best friend can feel like when you're in detention and if one of you even looks at the other the wrong way, you're gonna crack up.

Also, I may not be by nature a very sexual person. I hate being vulnerable, and intimate, or as promiscuous as my parents, who I assume have fucked more people than will buy this book. My husband doesn't exactly help the cause when he says things like, "Smell my hands, do they smell at all like poop to you?" One day, he called me into the bathroom, beaming with pride to show me that he had shit my initials in the toilet. He has pulled tampons out of my vagina and farted into my mouth while I'm half asleep for his own amusement.

Not that *all* of that isn't *super hot*. It's just not exactly the kind of behavior that sets you up for an orgasm. So for sixteen bucks, I decided what the hell and bought the book.

Maybe it was the graphic sex. Or the graphic sex, or the graphic sex. I really can't be sure. But within two days, I was finished with the first book and more sexually charged than I'd been since ever. My husband's cock was a walking bull's-eye. Of course, there are a million places online to find erotica far more sophisticated than E. L. James's classic, "He touched me down there." But the reason this book works is because it makes you wait for the payoff. And though nothing makes me more frustrated than waiting, the waiting is the best part. I think we often fail to recognize that by physically acting out our carnal desires, we are in that moment taking a chip out of the mountain of lust that got us there in the first place. Like every TV show from *X-Files* to *Sex and the City,* the minute the two main characters get together, we stop giving a fuck. Not to be a buzzkill, but kind of the hottest thing about sex is not having it. It's sort of like cocaine. The first bump is mind-blowing but from there, it's sadly downhill. And it's only at the end of the night, when you find yourself sweating from your head in some weirdo's studio apartment in Palms pretending to give a fuck about his exercise blog, that you realize your initial high is *never coming back.*

I think anyone who is in a relationship lasting longer than three months has in some way chosen comfort over butterflies. That being said, I think each of us yearns to feel those crazy, psychotic, "Oh my God the sky is falling" pangs that come from a series of first encounters. And that's what this book was able to give me. A vicarious feeling of newness and longing for a man who I'd seen eat his own earwax.

"What has gotten into you?" Jason asked one Sunday morning as I trapped him in our car outside a child's bris, begging him to finger me with a Pellegrino bottle I'd found under my seat.

"I've turned over a new leaf. A sex leaf," I said, unbuttoning my shirt.

"Awesome! Let's do this when we aren't in someone's front yard, yeah? God, this book really did a number on you," he said, extricating his penis from my ravenous grasp.

Before you run out and get a copy for yourself, know this:

The book is not good by any sort of literary standard. There is practically zero story. The heroine, Ana, is a fucking loser whom I'd never be friends with. And the love interest, Christian, is the type of guy who'd no doubt ask to fist me at a dinner party. My response, of course, being: "Dude, you're twenty-seven years old. Get the fuck away from me. . . . Wait, you have your own helicopter? Okay, come back."

The "story," such as it is, revolves around the dynamics of a BDSM (Bondage & Discipline/Sadism & Masochism) relationship, something I'd be hard-pressed to seek out in real life. Discipline tops my list of most hated things, followed closely by portobello mushrooms and actors.

My father is a control freak and my mom is Cher from the movie *Mermaids.* Regardless of whose roof I was under, nothing was up to me. I was either being groomed for my future eating disorder by being told that I hate watermelon because it has too much sugar in it, or being left at a movie theater because my mom temporarily forgot she had kids. If a guy tried to tie me up, I'd probably freak out and preemptively bludgeon my seducer to death with his own butt plug.

Luckily, the BDSM merely provided entrée into a larger world of role-play and fantasy. The whips and chains weren't the real turn-on; it was the power play leading up to them. The book initially hooked me with a scene in which Christian shows up at a bar miles away from where he's purported to be, to swoop in and save Ana from a drunken encounter with an aggressive friend. It sounds absurd even writing about it now, but deep down I think every woman (including myself) is looking for her white knight. And when that white knight does something really white knight-ish but then refuses to fuck you, you kind of want to gnaw your own arm off after masturbating yourself out of an anger tantrum.

In real life, when you first meet someone, you can project all sorts of bullshit narratives onto them to suit your fancy. However, once you are married, that leeway goes out the window. There's no room for a new story. You know the story.

By no means am I trying to dissuade you from getting married. I feel like the luckiest girl in the world to have my husband. But the hard truth is: You can't have both. Eventually a woman has to choose between deep, meaningful, occasionally platonic love and hot, dangerous, "Please don't break my heart, because I know you probably are hiding another family" sex.

Most men can pop in a low-grade porn and get hard the second they see a faceless pussy staring back at them. But women require more mental stimulation. We want a story to get wrapped up in. That's why whenever I watch porn with my husband, I insist we sit through the beginning narrative. *Look, if I'm gonna care about two dudes coming on a chick's face at the same time, I at least need to understand how they all know each other.*

Oscar Wilde said: "Everything in the world is about sex, except for sex. Sex is about power." E. L. James knows about the importance of the power/sex dynamic. She understands that the hottest thing about fucking someone's brains out is the psychological chess game you had to play—and win—to get there. Long story short: E. L. James is a hero. She is a goddamn humanitarian—and pretty much the Robin Hood of female libidos.

After zipping through *Fifty Shades Darker,* the second book in the trilogy, I was doing things I hadn't done in years, like shaving all the blond hairs off the back of my thighs, closing the bathroom door when I peed, and seducing my husband with more than just a simple: "I feel like we're supposed to be having sex." I was a rabid, insatiable animal. And by that I mean I wanted sex more than twice a week.

Hot as things had become between me and my husband, something was still missing. Despite our best efforts, we still weren't like the characters in the book. I was talking too much, and Jason's hitting me over the head with a pillow felt more like he was trying to suffocate me so he could go back to playing with his iPad. Christian and Ana also had things that we didn't have.

What is a sexual deviant without toys? I thought one afternoon while taking photos of my labia to send to him at work.

Admittedly, I go through phases where I get super passionate about something, throw myself 100 percent into whatever it is, and then ditch the whole thing a couple weeks later, when I'm waylaid by the next shiny object. And for the most part, my husband has always been supportive, even though the outcome is usually just me wasting a bunch of money on shit I end up giving to my maid's daughters. Like when I went through my whole Nag Champa–burning, meditation-crystal-collecting, vision-board phase. Or when I got an arm tattoo, then freaked out that it made me look like a biker and started getting it lasered off. Or when I took up pole dancing and hired a guy sitting outside Home Depot to come over and turn our guest bedroom into a "champagne room" one night while Jason was on Ambien. Exciting as it was initially, that phase ended rather abruptly when I busted my knee, reenacting the scene from *Striptease* where Rumer Willis walks out on stage in the middle of her mom's routine, resulting in a tit-heavy meltdown as Demi realizes the negative impact her lifestyle is having on her family and her soul. (Don't worry: I always made Jason play the kid.)

Knowing full well where my overzealous nature could lead, I tried hard to stay rational as I sped into the parking lot of my local sex store.

My heart started racing the moment I got out of the car. No matter what your age, a sex shop has this uncanny ability to make you feel like you are about to get busted for every depraved thing you've ever done. Holding my sunglasses tightly between my teeth, I walked through the front door.

Before this, I went to sex shops only to buy slutty Halloween costumes, and batteries for my mom's vibrators. This visit, however, was of a completely different nature. With determination, I walked past the sexy schoolgirl outfits and Pocket Rockets disguised as lipsticks and marched directly to the hardcore shit. I was browsing through the bondage aisle, filling my arms with weapons of mass seduction, when I came upon something called a "spreader bar." Looking at the price, I gasped.

Three hundred bucks? I have a whole dungeon to decorate!

"Excuse me," a voice chimed in behind me.

Guiltily, I turned around.

It had to be so obvious from the looks of me (nonthreatening person over thirty donning a wedding ring) and the contents of my arms (bondage fuck fest) that I was reading *Fifty Shades*.

"Would you like a basket?" a salesgirl asked, like we were at fucking Whole Foods. I hate how calm sex shop workers are, as if sex is the easiest thing to talk about in the world. I'm sure during training they get coached into talking about clits the way some people talk about coffeepots, but the rest of society doesn't operate that way. And I just find it a little stressful to have someone looking at me with a straight face while asking questions like, "Have you ever tried an ass egg?"

By the end of my supermarket sweep, I'd settled on one ass

egg, forgiving nipple clamps, some reasonably priced cock rings, two giant vibrators, a latex bodysuit, and a blindfold. On my way to the register, I noticed some small golden orbs sitting in a case near the glass dildos. They were Ben Wa balls. In *Fifty Shades,* James writes about similar balls in a steamy scene where Christian forces Ana to insert them into her vagina and wear them to a black tie event.

Fun! I thought, grabbing a pair and tossing them into my basket of vices. The heavily pierced girl behind the register nodded approvingly at my choices, tested the batteries in my new Rabbit Pearl, instructed me on how to clean my gimp suit, and then rung me up.

Back in my car, I was already plotting how I was going to ravage my husband. I felt like Wile E. Coyote mapping out a plan to capture the Road Runner and then ass-egg him to death.

When I got home, I did what I always do when I've gone shopping. I ripped the tags off everything and put it all on. I danced around the room in pain, trying to acclimate to the teeth on my new nipple clamps, then busted out the strange gold balls and shoved them inside my vagina. They were cold and heavy and kind of made me feel like I had two super-plus blood-drenched tampons in at once. Feeling both pride and shame that my vagina was wide enough to fit both balls, I tiptoed around the room, waiting to have some sort of Sting–Trudi Styler tantric cum explosion.

Just then, I heard the garage door opening. My husband was home! And was he in for a treat!

I threw a pair of boxers and a T-shirt over my bondage gear and ran downstairs to greet him, like any good dominant/submissive wife with a surprise might do.

The front door swung open, and I was suddenly face-to-face with my husband and an uptight, Aryan Youth–looking business acquaintance named Judd who kind of reminded me of the villain from the *The Karate Kid*.

Perhaps it was the surprise of seeing a near-stranger when I had XXX-rated plans in mind; perhaps it was my bouncing down the stairs; or perhaps my vagina was just that fucking big, but at that moment, my body decided it was time to purge the balls. I stood there, speechless, watching my pussy turn into a gumball machine.

Bap . . . Bap.

The metal balls hit the hardwood and rolled into the kitchen, only to find my innocent housekeeper, Lita.

"What the fuck!" Judd screamed like he'd just witnessed a home birth.

My husband's jaw hung open in horror as I charged after the orbs and ducked into the kitchen.

"Feels like maybe this is a bad time . . . ," I could hear Judd whisper to Jason as I scampered after my miscarried Ben Wa babies.

By the time I got to the kitchen, Lita already had one in hand.

"Oh! You can just throw those in the sink," I said, trying to play it cool.

I shamefully slunk back upstairs and waited for my husband to come ask me what the fuck was going on. I didn't see him until three hours later, when he eventually walked in, holding the balls.

"Lita was under the impression that these could go in the dishwasher," he said, smiling at me the way people smile at dogs and old people.

"Are you mad?"

"Mmm. No," he said.

"Can I whip you?"

"No."

Then he got in bed next to me and pulled me close. "You know what's hotter than you dressed as a scary dominatrix doing vagina parlor tricks for my friends?"

"What?" I asked coyly.

"Everything," he sighed, and then kissed me on the mouth intensely.

It was another phase, come and gone, and yet again, my husband managed to survive. The Ben Wa balls went the way of the stripper pole (to my maid's daughters), and our sex life returned to once a week. Sure, there's the rare night that I turn over in bed and wish I were staring at anybody else. But I think that's normal. And let's be real, would anybody else be able to shit my initials? I think not.

11.

Nobody Wants to Be Your Fucking Bridesmaid

Well, some girls do. But those are also usually the friends you keep around because they aren't as cute as you, have no significant other, and would brush your hair with their teeth if asked. I am not that girl, especially for my sister. It's not just because I'm cuter than her, it's also because I don't plan events.

When women ask you to be in their weddings, they might as well just say, "give me a check for a thousand dollars and all your attention for the next six months." But they don't. Instead, they try to spin it, making you feel like a giant honor is being bestowed upon you. When the reality is, it's all leading up to you looking pregnant on Facebook in a fucked-up empire waist dress from J.Crew bridal.

My sister, Amanda, asked me to be her maid of honor less because she wanted to and more because she'd been mine. She knew getting into it that I wasn't good with booking reservations, sending invitations, or talking numbers with anyone who knows how to add or subtract. But she asked anyway, probably because she knew that if anything went awry, she could fall back on her girlfriend Sheri.

Sheri was the girl who'd give Amanda a cat bath with her

tongue if called upon to do so. They met five years prior, when they were both assistants at a modeling agency, and became fast friends, bonding primarily over the fact that they both loved Amanda. If Amanda needed a ride to the airport, Sheri was there. If Amanda needed someone to watch her do jury duty, Sheri took three days off work. I always appreciated Sheri's involvement because it often meant less work for me.

Unlike me, Amanda was a traditional bride. She insisted on having an engagement party, a bridal shower, a bachelorette party, pre-wedding drinks, and a post-wedding brunch.

"Sheri is eager to get started on either my bachelorette or my shower. Which one do you want to throw?" Amanda asked one night over the phone.

To be honest, I wasn't particularly interested in throwing either. Both seemed like a clusterfuck to plan, and both events meant being on group e-mails with Sheri. An e-mail exchange with Sheri is like Chinese handcuffs, or maybe a Turkish prison: Once you are in, you are never getting out. She goes off topic and has to have the last word, even if that last word is just a series of emojis winking at each other. If I didn't choose, however, I'd find myself in a worse position: getting phone calls from Sheri. In haste, I opted for the bachelorette because I didn't really know what a bridal shower was, and at a bachelorette I could at least get away with pinning a dick on Sheri.

A month went by, and I did little more than buy edible penis necklaces and a heat lamp for the backyard. Then one night I got a crazed text from Sheri.

"Change of plans. I've convinced Amanda to do Vegas for the bachelorette! I'll hook you up with rooms at Planet Hollywood!"

Before I could respond, a flash mob of emojis exploded on my screen. What I assume was supposed to be five girls flying to Las Vegas looked instead like three Arabs and two tap-dancing twins crashing into the World Trade Center.

"I have work events every weekend this month, so I won't be able to go, but you guys are gonna rock it out! Woot, Woot," she wrote, followed by a champagne flute ejaculating onto a girl who just stabbed herself in the head with a pair of scissors.

After some consideration, I decided Vegas wouldn't be any less annoying than throwing a bash at my house. I was going to be stuck entertaining my sister regardless. In Vegas, I could escape to my own hotel room when she started referring to her vagina as her "hoo-hoo."

Since I was hosting, I insisted we invite my best friend, Simone, and my sister-in-law Veronica. Always looking for any excuse to pour herself into a bandage dress, Simone jumped at the opportunity. Veronica wasn't planning on flying to L.A. to hang out with "a bunch of uptight cunts whose parents paid for college," but as soon as she heard I was taking the cunts to Vegas, she too was in.

Amanda asked six girls, three of whom accepted: Ruthie, Roxy, and Garabaldo.

Garabaldo obviously wasn't her first name; it was Maxine, but she went by Garabaldo because people refused to call her anything else. Garabaldo was short and voluptuous with a huge personality that was eclipsed only by the size of her earrings. She liked doing things in excess—drinking, eating, talking. She was Amanda's freshman-year dormmate at Cal State Long Beach and the type of hot mess who instead of sleeping in her bed usually just passed out on a pile of hangers and shoes.

Ruthie and Roxy were sisters. They lived across the hall from Amanda and me when we tried living together for a year.

They were homebodies, partly because their third roommate was a three-foot-tall homegrown cannabis plant. Ruthie was blond like Amanda, with big Texas hair made bigger by Jessica Simpson clip-ins. Roxy was five years older. She was the type of girl you'd expect to meet on a beach in Thailand, carving Jerry Garcia's face into a log of driftwood.

Amanda decided to drive out with Ruthie and Roxy, which sounded like a fucking nightmare to Simone and me. We booked flights on Southwest and told the caravan to call us when they hit the Strip. Garabaldo was already in Vegas for a family graduation, and Veronica was flying in from Jersey that afternoon.

When we got to the hotel, the front desk clerk informed me that we had only one room reserved. Reluctantly, I called Sheri.

"Fuck. Everyone said just get one suite. Weren't you on that group e-mail? I think you might have me accidentally blocked," she said.

I pretended I couldn't hear her inside the casino and hung up.

Simone and I contemplated springing for our own room but then decided against it—because we were cheap and because we didn't want anyone else to benefit from our generosity.

The "suite" was a half-remodeled two-bedroom with kitchenette. In its previous incarnation, it was part of the Aladdin hotel—in diametric opposition to the Freddy Krueger claw and *Basic Instinct* poster now mounted above the "flying carpet" sofa. The hotel's remodel started in 2003 and was being done piecemeal. And though the lobby and public spaces were completely renovated, most of the guest rooms still made you feel like you'd been abducted by an autograph collector from Marrakech.

Before we could settle in, there was a knock at the door.

It was the rest of our group. Amanda, Roxy, and Ruthie marched in and started scoping out the beds. Behind them trailed Garabaldo, dragging three coffin-sized Louis Vuitton–esque trunks.

"How did you miss Garabaldo, Jenny?" Amanda said. "She was sitting in the lobby, waiting for you guys."

The truth was, it was hard to recognize Garabaldo. She'd lost nearly forty pounds since the last time I saw her.

"I guess I do look a little different." She laughed, lunging toward me and smearing neon orange lipstick across my cheek. Giant tugboats dangled from her earlobes, slapping her shoulders whenever she turned too fast. Even with the weight loss, Garabaldo still managed to look like a rich widow from Boca Raton on the verge of a nervous breakdown.

"Um, there are only three beds in this suite!" Ruthie shouted from the other room.

Quickly, as if they were playing a game of musical chairs, Amanda, Ruthie, and Roxy threw their bags on top of a bed. Lucky for me, Simone was already topless and reading an *Us Weekly* in one of them.

"Sorry, already occupied. Jenny? You're my plus-one," she said, not looking up but patting the spot beside her like she was summoning a lapdog.

Ruthie grimaced and walked into the other room to share a bed with her sister.

Before Garabaldo could saddle up next to Amanda, she was banished to the pullout in the living room.

"I kick and thrash around all night. It's best I don't have anyone next to me," Amanda said, taking Garabaldo's things off the nightstand and handing them back to her.

Once Garabaldo was ousted, the girls closed their bedroom

door to smoke weed. The party hadn't even started, and lines in the sand were already being drawn. We were like three separate tribes on *Survivor*: Amanda and the sisters versus me and Simone versus Garabaldo and whatever dead bodies she was hiding in her luggage.

"I'm already bored and Garabaldo weirds me the fuck out," Simone whispered as she popped a Percocet and a Tic Tac.

"Look, once Veronica arrives, the whole dynamic is going to shift. She loves everybody and everybody loves her." I texted Veronica and told her to meet us at the Mandalay Bay pool.

The little research I'd done indicated that the cabanas at Mandalay were the best in town. Upon arriving, we quickly learned why.

"WHAT. THE. FUCK. Everybody is fucking naked!" Ruthie covered her face appalled as we approached the pool at the Mandalay. A lubed-up Latino escorted us to our cabana and took our drink order.

"Two White Russians, and do you guys serve fries?" Roxy asked through bloodshot eyes.

"What's a White Russian?" Garabaldo said.

"The best drink ever! Bring three. And onion rings," Ruthie said.

The thought of someone devouring a basket of onion rings and washing it down with a cream-based beverage paralyzed me with fear for a good five seconds. I ordered a water with lemon. Under normal circumstances, I love watching people around me get fat. But at a topless pool, it just seemed inhumane.

Simone strutted off to the bathroom in six-inch heels and a bikini that screamed "cum on my face." When she returned, her tits were out and flapping in the wind.

"Am I the only one who's gonna follow the rules here?"

Ruthie and Roxy stared out from under their beach towel blankets in disgust.

"These are great!" Garabaldo hollered, slamming back her first White Russian.

Three hours and twelve White Russians later, Ruthie and Roxy were passed out; Simone was in the hot tub with three Australian dudes playing a game of "guess where my implant incisions are"; and Amanda was wandering around, asking if anyone had seen Garabaldo.

"Hey, bitches!" a voice called out from behind. It was Veronica.

"I just walked past a wasted chick floating in the deep end with only one eye open. Do you think I should tell someone?" she asked.

Just then, the lubed Latino returned.

"I'll take a rum and Coke." Veronica lit a menthol and took her shoes off.

"I'm sorry, but we are going to have to ask your friend to leave," he said to us.

"I don't think you can smoke—," I started.

"Not that friend, the one sleeping in the pool. She's a liability."

On the other side of the pool, Amanda hung off the diving board, trying to prod Garabaldo awake with a net. Garabaldo giggled, half-conscious, bobbing up and down like a buoy. Her face was underwater now, save for one open eye blinking up at us like a crocodile.

"That fucking mess is with us?" Veronica asked, ashing her menthol on a tray of finished drinks being carted by.

Once we fished Garabaldo out of the pool, we hailed a cab and headed back to our hotel. "I think she needs her stomach pumped," Ruthie said, trying to hold Garabaldo steady as we walked through the lobby. Her wet body slipped through our hands and slid across the marble floor as we made our way back to our suite. It was as though we were carrying an adult seal wearing eyeshadow.

Amanda was annoyed and already bitching about how none of this would be happening if Sheri had planned her bachelorette.

"My friends aren't comfortable being nude in public, Jenny! No wonder Garabaldo got wasted. She probably didn't know how else to deal with the pressures of being a whore."

"Look, we're gonna go out to a nice dinner, maybe a club, do some gambling." I tried to calm her down.

"Having a bachelorette party is all about being a whore!" Veronica barked through a cloud of menthol smoke. "In Jersey, you'd all be covered in dick by now."

"Umm, I don't think cigarettes are allowed in the elevator," Amanda coughed, furiously pressing the button for our floor.

"*What the—! Jesus! Fuck!* Are you kidding me?" Veronica shouted, reading a text off her phone.

Simone shot me a look and mimed blowing her brains out.

"What is it?" Amanda asked.

"My fucking landlord is trying to get me evicted because of my cat! He's a Persian so he's extremely vocal."

"Your landlord?" Roxy asked.

"My cat. My cat is Persian. My landlord is just some chink asshole." She stomped her feet, causing the elevator cables to bounce.

The doors opened, and two Asian businessmen stepped in. There were now nine people in the elevator. Three of whom were wet and two of whom I hoped didn't hear the word "chink." I debated jumping out, but we had over fifteen flights to go.

As soon as the elevator started moving, the men realized they made a mistake—their intention was to go downstairs, not up. They exchanged a few unintelligible words under their breath and waited patiently as we continued to ascend.

With barely enough room to flex her arm, Veronica scrolled through her phone and called her landlord.

" Hi! What the fuck are you even talking about? Speak English! No, he's not there alone! He has a sitter, and why the fuck are you peering through my windows anyway? Call the police! I dare you! Do it! I hope they arrest your illegal ass you stupid fucking asshole motherfucking chink!"

The Asian men turned around in horror.

"It's a Jersey thing. They'll all be friends again in twenty to thirty minutes," I said, mortified.

Then, Garabaldo opened her mouth and heaved up a thick layer of onion rings, White Russians, and diet pills all over Amanda.

"Jenny!" Amanda screamed.

"What am I doing?"

Before Amanda could blame me for Garabaldo's intoxication, her digestive tract, and her lifelong battle with her weight, the doors opened on our floor.

Desperate for air, we trampled over the Asian businessmen and ran to our suite.

Roxy and Ruthie rolled a joint while Amanda jumped in the shower with entitlement, leaving Garabaldo and her vomit-encrusted body to rot on the sofa. Veronica stayed in the hallway, smoking and waiting for her catsitter to call her back.

"Where would you rank this on worst vacations of your life . . . ?" Simone said, trailing off as she noticed Garabaldo dog-crawl from the couch to the kitchenette in search of a snack.

Everyone was miserable. The weekend was unraveling around us, and there was only one thing that could save it: male strippers. I Googled "stripper police officers" because, let's be honest, firemen all have mustaches. Simone picked out the ones she'd consider getting fingered by and placed an order.

Once Amanda was out of the shower, she asked Ruthie and Roxy to throw Garabaldo in and hose her down. The girls obliged. I peered into the hallway to check on Veronica, who seemed to be cooling off. She spoke to her sitter and all was well. She also pointed out that in the heat of her rage, she punched the fire extinguisher by the elevator and that if anything was broken, I'd need to pay for it. The crew assembled in the living room, and I laid out the plan.

"We are going to dinner, doing a few craps tables, then coming back to the room for other surprises which will be divulged when the time is right," I said. I was beaming with pride.

"It better not be strippers," Amanda smiled, clearly hoping it was strippers.

Dinner was uneventful—aside from the fact that we all donned penis necklaces—and it only helped to underscore the fact that our group shared zero common interests. Garabaldo was conscious again and already nursing her second post-throw-up White Russian.

"These are totally my drink now!" She laughed as one of her false eyelashes crept down her face, giving her a stroke victim's gaze.

"So, who wants to know details about my future husband's pee-pee?" Amanda said, dead sober.

None of us did. Amanda waited for a response, then launched into a detailed account of her sex life past and present. She giggled, entertained by her own story as if somebody else were telling it to her. She sipped on a glass of champagne and would whisper conspiratorially whenever she used the word "fuck." The group smiled sympathetically, which only encouraged greater detail.

The meal ended how all group meals end, in a passive-aggressive standoff. Everybody insisted they'd paid, but we were still one hundred dollars short on the bill. Ruthie nudged Garabaldo, who was again properly wasted.

"Baldo, you sure you paid? I didn't see you open your—"

Baldo cut her off by breaking into drunken hysterics. By now, the moving eyelash was resting just above her lip like a fake mustache.

"Why does everybody hate me!?" she screamed, and ran off to the bathroom carrying the few last sips of her White Russian with her.

Everybody chipped in a few more bucks and waited patiently for her return. After twenty minutes, Amanda stood up, demanding we leave.

"Well, why don't you drag your friend and whatever's left of her makeup out of the bathroom?" Veronica said. She was still pissed that she had paid over fifty dollars for a personal pizza and two martinis.

Offended, Amanda marched off to the bathroom. Simone started stress-eating her penis necklace, and Roxy looked like she was about to fall asleep. Five minutes passed before Amanda returned alone.

"Where's Garabaldo?" I asked.

"She's not in there."

"What do you mean? Where is she?"

"I don't know, Jenny! God!" She had reverted back into the fifteen-year-old version of herself.

"Then what took you so long?" Veronica pushed.

Amanda looked around, beet red. "I was pooping. Okay?"

With the mention of pooping, the waiter walked back over and promptly asked us to leave. "We're gonna need this table for another party, sooo . . ." He was using his fake-nice voice.

"Um, actually, we're missing someone. The girl who was sitting on the end," I said.

He shook his head, clearly not recalling.

"She wanted Equal packets for her White Russian?" Ruthie offered.

Still nothing.

"I'm covering ten tables per hour, I really don't have time to remember faces." The waiter spoke about his job with the kind of gravitas usually reserved for doctors working the ER.

The group got up and we all headed back to the bathroom to do a final check. Ruthie dialed Baldo's cell, but it went straight to voice mail.

"She's not here. And that was definitely the stall you shit in," Veronica said, walking out of a stall and lighting an incense match from inside her purse.

We decided to go up to the room to see if maybe Garabaldo was hiding under a blanket or dead in the bathtub, covered in pills. When we arrived, the cops were already knocking on our door.

"Excuse me? Can we help you?" Amanda asked, concerned.

"Yes, we had a complaint. Are you Amanda Mollen?" the first cop asked.

"Oh Jesus! She's dead, isn't she?" Veronica lit another menthol and slid down a wall, shocked.

I tried to remain calm and position myself to look like the sane one of the group. "What exactly happened, officers?"

"I think we need to discuss this inside," Cop Number Two chimed in.

Ruthie had the keys, so she opened the door. We all closed our eyes for fear that Garabaldo might be hanging from the ceiling.

Once inside, Cop Number One's tone changed. "I'm Officer Brooks and this is my partner, Officer Perez. Amanda Mollen? You are under arrest."

Brooks grabbed Amanda and cuffed her. "You have the right to remain silent."

"What are you doing?" Ruthie cried out.

"And you have the right to remain *sexy*." Brooks pushed Amanda down on the couch and straddled her. "Pour Some Sugar on Me" by Def Leppard started blasting out of Perez's bag.

Both men ripped off their uniforms, giving way to tiny sock-stuffed Speedos.

"Stop! *Nooo!*" Amanda screamed, kicking an undulating Perez away from her crotch.

"Umm, excuse me, guys, sorry," I interrupted. "But we have a slight problem on our hands." I tried to avoid eye contact with Brooks, who was still face-fucking my sister.

"Let me guess," Perez said, picking up his pants, defeated. "You want firemen."

"No. No. No. You're perfect. There's absolutely nothing wrong with you guys. And you're doing a great job, it's just we have a friend who's missing and—"

"It's just not the right time to be getting our pussies eaten," Veronica said, cutting to the chase.

Ruthie and Roxy scanned the rest of the suite for signs of Garabaldo.

"I don't think she was here." Roxy walked around the room like a dog sniffing out a bomb.

"I think we should go talk to the front desk," Amanda

said, shimmying out of her plastic handcuffs and away from Brooks's sock-cock.

"We're coming with you," Perez said directly to Simone's tits.

The eight of us walked through the lobby with purpose. Neither Brooks nor Perez had a change of clothes that wasn't a banana hammock, so they had no choice but to stay in uniform.

Amanda and I approached a red-haired concierge who was busy playing some sort of prepubescent iPhone game.

"Hi, I need to report a missing person," Amanda said.

"Umm. Is this person missing or are you just split up?" he asked.

Amanda looked at me, confused. The truth was, we didn't actually know if Baldo was missing, per se. She could have just been pissed off, wandering around the food court, or stuck in a high-stakes craps game as the designated dice kisser.

"Why don't you give us a description and a phone number, and we'll call you if we see her. Big groups get split up all the time."

We took turns rattling off a rough description of Baldo.

"Okay, umm, sort of stout," I said.

"Big hair," Amanda chimed in.

"One eyelash."

"RuPaul makeup."

"Penis necklace. Oh, and was last seen carrying a White Russian." I was certain I'd just cracked the case wide open.

"Can you describe the Russian?"

"Small. Like two or three sips left."

"It's a drink. Not a person," Amanda barked.

The concierge looked back at our group, then again at us. He leaned over his desk and whispered, "You know those guys aren't real cops, right?"

"Yes. We know." We turned and walked off self-consciously, like we'd just been caught leaving our twenty-two-year-old neighbor's apartment at 6 A.M.

Once we rejoined our group, we told them the situation.

"Before we can report Baldo missing," Amanda explained, "we have to try to look for her."

"Wait, you guys haven't looked for this girl yet?" Perez pulled away, like someone in a position to judge others' life choices.

"We called her cell," Roxy said, defensive.

"I'm sure she hasn't gotten far. She has a blood alcohol level of roughly .20 and really short legs." Veronica lit her last menthol, offering to share it with Brooks.

Ruthie and Roxie felt someone needed to call hospitals and wait in the room in case Baldo returned. Perez grabbed Simone and volunteered to search neighboring hotels. Amanda, Brooks, and I took the casino while Veronica offered to go buy herself more menthols.

The three of us walked the casino for hours into the early morning.

"This could be the worst night of my life, you know." Amanda sat at a slot machine and started to cry.

"I'm really sorry. I thought I was planning something you'd enjoy. I never expected things to get so utterly fucked." I tried to hug her, but it got awkward when Brooks piled on top.

"Aw, guys, if it makes you feel any better, I worked a party last week where a lady got a microphone stuck in her vagina."

Just then, my cell rang. It was Roxy.

"Do you have her?" I asked.

"No, but the rest of us are up in the room stoned. Oh and I'm pretty sure your friend and Officer Perez are fucking on your side of the bed as we speak. Do you guys wanna get breakfast?"

Amanda's feet were bulging out of her Barbie-pink Louboutins like she was having an allergic reaction. Whether she wanted to or not, her body was telling her it was time to stop.

A hostess reunited us with the rest of our search party at a large booth in a nearby diner. Veronica, Roxy, and Ruthie were stoned. Simone was braided around Perez like a friendship bracelet and demanded we sit down.

"Why do you guys look so miserable?" Simone asked as Perez dropped an ice cube down the front of her shirt.

"Well, we came here with six girls and we're going home with five, for starters," I said.

"I'm sure she's going to turn up," Perez said. "She most likely fell asleep somewhere. Did you tell them about the chick last week who got the microphone lodged in her hoo-hoo?" He looked up at Brooks, who nodded yes.

I ordered pancakes, hash browns, and a side of french fries and tried to forget about a future, specifically one where anybody referred to a vagina as a "hoo-hoo"

"If anyone asks how this weekend went, can we all agree to lie? I have some people I need to impress on Facebook." Veronica pulled out a compact and started fixing her makeup for a selfie.

We all agreed that lying made the most sense. Amanda wanted to make sure her fiancé, Larry, thought she enjoyed herself as much as he did at his bachelor party. I wanted to look like someone responsible enough to organize an event. And Simone wanted to avoid the reality that she had "sort of" protected sex with a male stripper.

Maybe it was in honor of Baldo, or maybe it was because there was still male stripper cum all over our sheets, but I woke up that morning on the floor covered in hangers and shoes. The rest of the group was awake and sitting in the living room. When I walked out, Baldo was sitting with them. She was in the exact same outfit she left us in only now it was splattered with blood and ranch dressing. The forty pounds she'd recently lost she seemed to have gained back overnight. Her one eyelash was still attached, and her hair looked like it got teased and set on fire.

"Baldo! What the fuck happened to you last night?" I really wanted to say, "I thought you were dead, cunt!"

Baldo packed her trunks for the airport as she launched into a crazy story about her dysfunction with men, her overbearing mother, and how she accidentally won three grand playing blackjack. She didn't remember the night in detail and only knew where she'd gone based on the chips still in her pocket. She said she woke up in a hotel room fully clothed next to an elderly man and his wife, who helped her get in a cab and find her way home. She also recalled winning a giant stuffed animal on the ring toss at Circus Circus but then traded it to a family outside the Hard Rock in exchange for the rest of a corn dog. The blood was from her nose, which she attributed to her high blood pressure. As for the ranch, she had no idea.

Brooks and Perez were long gone, and the suite looked like Simone's future abortion. The rest of us gathered up our personal belongings and headed downstairs, hoping to return to the lives we had before. In the elevator, each of us reflected silently. Then just as we were about to reach the lobby, Amanda turned and faced the group.

"I really appreciate you guys coming here for me. It was a strong effort."

I couldn't help but be touched by my sister's graciousness.

"And I think it's probably best if we don't see each other again until the wedding," she continued.

The doors opened to the bustling lobby and we all went in separate directions. Ruthie, Roxy, and Amanda headed out to the parking lot. Simone and I hailed a cab to the airport with Veronica. And Baldo walked into the casino and let it envelop her, like someone taking their final suicidal steps into a vast ocean.

The fact that Baldo didn't die on my clock seemed like a win. I couldn't help but be slightly pleased with myself for pulling off a weekend that was at the very least memorable, if not perfect. And just like any good bachelorette party should do, the seven of us were bonded for it. Not because of our shared memories, but because we're still arguing about who should cover the hotel-room damages.

12.

Botoxic Shock Syndrome

Here's the deal, ladies–eventually we are all gonna look like our grandmothers. Everybody gets older. Everybody falls apart. And for most women, turning thirty means admitting that despite our best efforts to keep dating club promoters, wearing short shorts, and doing the occasional line of cocaine in a public restroom, we aren't kids anymore. Society and our weird uncles no longer look at us like nubile pieces of ass fresh out of college who can get away with not wearing bras. College was over ten fucking years ago, and your boobs look like shit.

It starts to dawn on you that people around you—driving cars, making deals, and dancing in cages—happen to be an entire generation younger. This displacement causes some of us to question where we fit in. We're not quite our mothers, but we also aren't the sheltered princesses whose fathers are still paying our rent. (Well, at least not all of it.) While we were settling into emo music, skinny jeans, and dye jobs that accentuated our roots, frown lines were settling into our faces, sunspots were showing up on our skin, and our ass cheeks decided to grow hair. For a lot of us, these changes were subtle enough to ignore. But even in great lighting, it's undeniable that middle age is on its way.

When you're an actor, the deck is shuffled even faster, and by twenty-eight, you're pretty much old enough to play Ben

Affleck's mom. One day, you're cast as the sexy girl next door, and the next, you're the crazy widow who wanders the cul-de-sac with her Ugg-boots-wearing dog. It's a harsh reality that a million miles on the elliptical and a thousand quarts of StriVectin can't undo. Culturally, whether we like it or not, young is beautiful and old is irrelevant. Now, I guess I could be one of those really strong women who embraces my wrinkles and lets one streak of hair go gray, but let's be honest, those women are annoying and probably don't wear deodorant. I wanna look cute until "cute" is pried from my cold dead fingers, and if that makes me a shallow bitch who allows mass media to dictate my self-worth, then I wear the title as a badge of honor.

At thirty-three (I'm thirty-four now, but let's pretend this chapter was written a few months ago back when I was still thirty-three because why not?), I feel like I've done everything under the sun to maintain my youth. I've been conned into ridiculous workout programs, manipulated into buying salt from the Dead Sea, and in my darkest hour, even let my hairdresser give me bangs. I wasn't at the point where I needed anything drastic, but I was at the point where when I looked in the mirror I saw my dad in a wig. That's where Botox came in.

Here's the deal with Botox: It's awesome. The only people who don't like it are people who don't get it—like my husband. He thinks freezing your face muscles with bacteria scraped from improperly handled meat products is a gateway procedure, and something that will eventually lead to surgery, and lasers, and me looking like Joan Rivers (which is completely ridiculous, since I was using lasers *way* before I discovered Botox). So in a selfless effort to appease him, I don't tell him about it. And aside from the one or two occasions when I pretended that the environmental stresses of our home life had resulted in a mild case of Bell's palsy, things have been pretty copacetic. My husband is happy and completely in the dark, and I look ever-so-slightly Photoshopped.

The fact that both my parents are body-conscious nut jobs probably didn't help my obsessive need for physical perfection. I'm also certain that watching both of them dabble in face work before forty did, in a way, anesthetize me to the idea that it could be dangerous to start young. I grew up with the understanding that I'd eventually need a second boob job after breastfeeding, the fat pads under my eyes removed when they started to look too bulbous, and a face-lift when I hit seventy. These were commonplace procedures that were just part of growing up. I always felt more or less blessed that I inherited my mother's Irish nose and my father's olive skin. I knew there would be things to fix in the future, but thankfully most of those things were minor.

At twenty-nine, I was the first of my friends to take the plunge with Botox, but over time, I've watched almost all of them succumb to the delicious temptation to stave off nature with injections. Americans spend over $50 billion per year on beauty. And as technology advances, so do our expectations. It's hard for even the strongest of us not to take advantage. It's like steroids in baseball. Sure, nobody is admitting to juicing, but the fact is, the players that are abstaining are finding themselves competing against the players that aren't. But the point of this essay isn't to encourage you to use steroids. It's to encourage you to use Botox—*if* and *when* you need it. In *small,* conservative doses. Administered by a licensed physician or really well-kempt nurse.

My friend Candice is one year older than me. She's one of those purists who never really bought in to the whole "fucking with her appearance" thing. She doesn't wear makeup, and her eyebrows naturally grow in a perfect arch. When she has a zit, she has the willpower not to touch it. When her hair is a mess, she twirls it into a ponytail and doesn't think about it again. She eats whatever she feels like. She works out when she has time. Candice is the type of chick I hate because everything about her is effortless. Nothing is forced or overthought. She's never had surgery, braces, or even colored her hair. What you see is what you get.

I met Candice for brunch one morning about six months ago (back when I was still thirty-three). After two hours of me bitching to her that my Instagram account was shut down because I posted a picture of my fingers between my legs, resembling a dick, I let her speak.

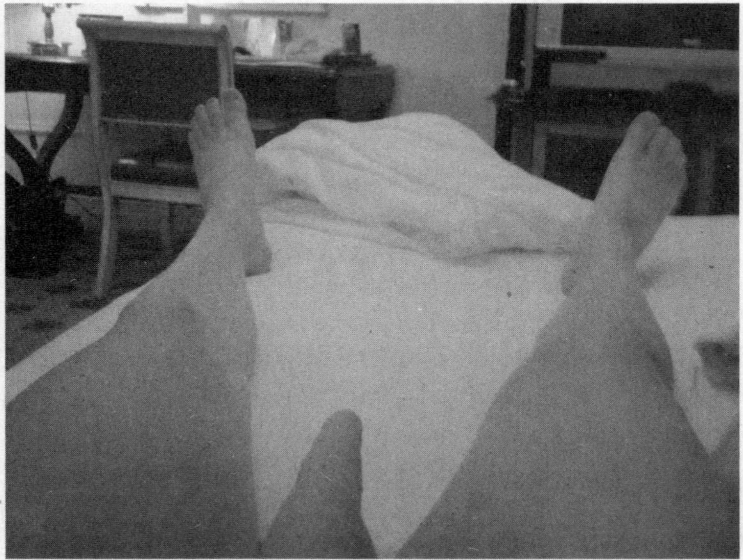

Finger dick.

"So, I think I want to get Botox," she said in an even tone that suggested she'd already made up her mind.

A warm soothing wave of validation washed over me. Candice, the most secure woman I knew, had things she wanted to change about herself. She looked great, but she wanted to look amazing—just like I did.

"What were you thinking you needed?" I asked, containing my excitement, as if she'd just said, "Let's take a bath in a tub of Nutella."

"I wanted to fill in these smile lines and maybe tweak this dent between my eyebrows." She seemed bashful but unflinching in her conviction.

I wasn't sure what changed Candice's stance on face work. Maybe her husband said the wrong thing, maybe she accidentally looked at herself in an airplane lavatory, or maybe she just started to appreciate the difference in the people around her. The catalyst was unclear, but I imagine it probably had to do with me looking amazing. So I offered to take her to my guy.

"I have the best guy! He looks a little waxy because he's done a few too many peels and I think he might have silicone implants in his lips, but other than that, he's the greatest."

"Cool," she said.

I reached across the table and started playing with her face like I was the doctor I'd just described.

"Okay, so first of all, your marionettes are going to need filler, not Botox."

"What are my marionettes?"

"You know, the lines around your mouth that make you look like a puppet." I grabbed her cheeks and pulled them back to give her a sense of what I was talking about.

"I look like a puppet?" Candice stared at me hard.

"No. Of course not!" I backpedaled. "Not like a real puppet. More like a person playing a puppet in a community theater production of *Pinocchio*. You know—like super creepy at first, but then you get used to it and sort of start to find it adorable."

Candice's smile lines slowly melted into even fiercer frown lines.

My explanation wasn't helping.

"They really aren't even that noticeable! Regardless, it's all going to go away as soon as we inject the filler."

"Filler? I just want a few drops of Botox. I don't want to get into all that fancy stuff." Candice grew more self-conscious by the moment.

It suddenly occurred to me that certain people, the ones who were loved unconditionally by their parents, can't always handle being picked apart physically. I needed to remember to be gentle with Candice and her glaringly obvious marionette lines.

"When do you want to go?" I pulled out my phone and started dialing.

"This week?" she suggested, rubbing her face.

Candice is a small-town girl from Iowa. Growing up, she was sheltered from the ways of the city and in many ways raised to be someone who'd never talk to me. When she first got to Los Angeles, simple things like hair extensions, teeth bleaching, and Brazilian waxes were foreign concepts to her. With time she became savvier but still refused to participate in the madness. Candice always got a kick out of hearing me go on about whatever latest craze I'd gotten myself mixed up in. And my ability to amuse her is most likely why she stuck around. Our Botox adventure was going to be the first time Candice wasn't just a passive listener on the other end of the phone. This time, she was going to be the one doing something she deemed outrageous, and there was no way I was going to miss it.

Taking Candice to her Botox appointment was what I picture taking a child to Disneyland must feel like for parents. I wanted to be there to help her feel better about herself, but also to vicariously experience the wonder that comes from seeing a couple cc's of Restylane shot under your skin for the first time.

I was able to get Candice an appointment with the famed Dr. Sorenson of Beverly Hills Dermatology three days later. When I picked Candice up from work, her palms were already sweating.

"Do you really think this is the right thing to do?" She pulled down the passenger-side mirror and furiously moved her eyebrows up and down.

"Candice, you are really overreacting. Nothing is going to happen." I drove down Beverly Drive, looking for the cheapest parking structure.

"Because my husband can never know I did this. Like, nobody can know I did this."

I pulled into the next lot and pulled a ticket out of the machine. "Your forehead isn't going to all of a sudden be smooth. The Botox won't set in for at least six or seven days."

"What about the filler?" she asked.

"Oh, that's immediate."

A dermatology office is like Planned Parenthood for the middle-aged. Nobody makes eye contact, nobody talks, and everyone is guilty of more than they are admitting. After several uneasy minutes of Candice making me swear on my dogs' lives that I would never tell Jason or even my dogs about our visit, a tall blond nurse who couldn't have been more than twenty-two walked out to greet us.

"Hi, I'm Kinga. I'm new here."

Kinga escorted us back to an exam room in tight black sweater pants that looked like they were made for a doll. The people in Dr. Sorenson's office were always beautiful, but Kinga was truly a specimen.

"So you're a regular?" she asked me.

I nodded my head yes and tried not to imagine Kinga getting railed by Dr. Sorenson on her lunch break.

She closed the door to our room and looked over Candice's chart.

"So what areas are we working on today?"

Candice looked at me, then again at the ever-so-slightly plastic twenty-something (who'd clearly already started her own journey down the rabbit hole of facial alterations), and said nothing.

"Don't worry, I'm not going to tell anyone. I just need to know where to apply the numbing cream." Kinga pulled an alcohol wipe from the cupboard and started cleaning Candice's face.

Once she finished, she left the room to get Dr. Sorenson.

Dr. Sorenson is a handsome, hyperactive narcissist of unspecified age who, over the course of the last decade, has become Los Angeles's uncrowned king of injectables.

"They call me the uncrowned king of injectables," he announced, strutting into the room like he was on a catwalk and extending his hand. Kinga followed closely behind.

"How you doing, Jenny? Did you meet Kinga?" He gave me a fist bump, then turned to Kinga for a black marker. She was definitely getting her face fucked off later that day.

Sorenson didn't ask Candice a single question. He just

drew. After Jackson Pollocking Candice's face the same way I envisioned him jizzing all over Kinga's, he held up a mirror.

"So this is what I would suggest. What did you have in mind?" he asked, only out of obligation.

"I—uh—," Candice stuttered as she took in what looked like a giant tribal face tattoo.

"We were really just thinking just some Restylane in her smile lines and a couple drops of Botox between the brows." I knew Candice wasn't ready for the works. She needed to be eased in slowly.

"Oh, is that what *you* were thinking?" Sorenson gave me a look that said, *I'm the motherfucking uncrowned king of injectibles, not you.*

"That work for you, Candice?" he asked sweetly.

"Well, um. Do you think I need more?"

Kinga cleaned the abstract expressionist rendering off Candice's face as Sorenson prepared his syringe of hope.

"Do I? Well, yeah. Frankly, I do. Take Kinga here. She's twenty-four and she is wearing more cc's of Botox than what you're requesting, and you look two times her age. You actually need it. She is just doing hers to be preventative."

"Preventative?" Candice wasn't following.

"Yeah, so she doesn't hit thirty-five and have the deep lines you do. Open your mouth." Sorenson positioned several fingers on the inside of her cheek and started injecting. "A girl like you has to act fast. Forty is just around the corner, and right now, you're not ready for it. Do you want to be ready for it?"

Candice tried to answer, but Sorenson's hand was in the way.

"Don't answer that." He massaged the gel-like substance

through her jowls with his fingers, then started on the opposite side.

As tears streamed down Candice's new face, I squeezed her hand tightly and assured her it was almost over.

Sorenson reached past Kinga, grabbed a separate syringe filled with Botox, and started injecting again. "I have a bit extra, so I'm just gonna put it in your crow's-feet. That okay with you, Jenny?"

"It's too late at this point," Candice said. "Just give me the works." She smiled almost giddily now.

Seconds later, he handed Candice back the mirror.

"Wow!" she said, blown away by the drastic effects of the filler.

"Now does that look like too much?" Sorenson laughed, pleased with his work and with himself in general. Before he left, he rattled off his routine advice.

"No exercise for the rest of the day, any slight bruising is normal, and if you have an adverse reaction, please call the office immediately."

Candice nodded, grateful.

"Looks like you're almost due to come back in, Jenny. You should book something before you leave." He couldn't resist taking one last jab at me.

Kinga walked us to the front desk, where Candice paid her bill in cash and reiterated that she didn't want anyone knowing she was there.

We drove back to Candice's work and I dropped her off. One part paranoid and one part elated, she hugged me hard and thanked me for being such a bad influence before getting out of the car. Though she clearly did look better and seemed as happy as could be, I couldn't help but feel like a drug dealer who'd just hooked a third-grader on heroin.

"You like to fly kid?" I imagined myself saying. "I'll teach you to fly."

That night, as I sat in bed taking iPhone pictures of my forehead so I could compare them with Google Images search results for "Klingon Halloween Masks," I found myself questioning my enthusiasm for corrupting my innocent friend.

"Sorenson was just trying to mindfuck me into giving him more money or killing myself," I grumbled to my dogs, forgetting I'd sworn on their lives I wouldn't tell them about taking Candice to the dermo.

When Jason came home, I spoke nothing of the occurrence. He asked about my day, I asked about his, and we fell asleep as best of friends, the kind who tell each other everything.

The next morning, I woke to a series of cryptic texts from Candice, urging me to call her immediately. Before I could get through all the messages, my home phone was ringing.

"Hello?"

Candice was sobbing, making it impossible to understand her.

"Are you okay? Is someone dead? Do I need Botox too?"

"My face!" she cried.

"What's wrong with your face?"

"I'm bruised right next to my eye! Nick is going to shoot me! I can't believe I let you talk me into this!"

"Hang on, I didn't talk you into it. You came to me with the idea."

"Hoping you would tell me I didn't need it!" I could hear Candice's dog yelp as she tripped over him and continued to pace neurotically.

Scared she might get behind the wheel of a car and try to

drive out of state, I told her I'd come over. I threw on some shoes and a bra and drove to her house. When I got there, she was wearing a huge hat with a fishnet veil on it that she'd made for the Kentucky Derby.

"Come in," she said, furtively glancing around her driveway, making sure nobody was watching.

Once we got to her bathroom, she unveiled herself. Her marionettes were completely gone, but just to the right of one eye was a pea-sized bruise. I assured her that it was minor and would last only a week.

"You just need some good concealer."

"Good concealer? I don't have any concealer!" she panicked.

Rummaging through my purse, I found a cover-up stick that was at least a shade too dark.

"You really want to have yellow to cover up blue . . . ," I said as I mixed in a dash of her husband's baby powder like a Caribbean witch doctor mixing a homemade tincture in a futile attempt to cure a patient's malaria.

I applied my makeshift mixture to the spot, hoping for the best. Unfortunately, it just made the discoloration more obvious.

Candice looked in the mirror and went back to freaking the fuck out.

"Now it looks even worse! Besides, Nick is going to be more skeptical if I'm wearing makeup! There has to be another way."

"Can you throw yourself down a flight of stairs?" I suggested helpfully. "Walk into an open cupboard while he's looking at you?" I tried to remember all the various ways I'd explained bruising in the past. Once, I made the mistake of trying collagen in my lips. My lips blew up to the size of inner tubes, so I told Jason I was having an allergic reaction to cantaloupe. The swelling got so bad that I eventually let him stab me in the butt with our emergency epinephrine pen just to avoid further questioning.

Candice was the type of girl who started breathing hard the minute she even attempted to do something nefarious. Any sort of elaborate lie might give her too much time to accidentally break down and confess. She needed a one- or two-word answer she could spit out while avoiding eye contact, and then change the subject.

"Let's think, what could you have done today that might have caused this?"

"Um, maybe something at the gym?"

"A needle attacked you at the gym? No way. It's too small to be a gym accident." I racked my brain thinking of plausible scenarios, but all I came up with was "misguided insulin shot," "misguided heroin needle," or "misguided extra in a remake of *Death Becomes Her*." Sadly, Candice wasn't a diabetic, a heroin junkie, or an actress/waitress. She was a woman nearing forty with crow's-feet I wouldn't have even mentioned if Sorenson hadn't opened his cosmetically enhanced duck lips.

"Jenny! Stop! It looks like a Botox bruise! That's all it's ever gonna look like." Candice sat down on her toilet, resigned. She didn't have any fight left in her.

"Not if we make it bigger," I said without thinking.

Life shot back into Candice's eyes. She stood up and grabbed my shoulders hard. "Will you punch me?" A small tear of desperation fell down her now-flawless cheek.

I thought about the Candice I'd known in my twenties—the strong, seemingly unaffected beauty who could barely be bothered to apply ChapStick. I thought about myself—the recovered anorexic who'd looked into having her anus bleached after catching a weird glimpse of it in a magnifying mirror in tenth grade. Maybe I'd projected too much of my own shit onto Candice. Maybe I should have asked more questions. Unfortunately, it was too late for questions. What was done was done.

"Please." She was begging now, closing her eyes slightly and bracing for impact.

Instantly I was transported back to the previous Christmas, where after an afternoon of sailing and snorkeling, my stepmom, Kristen, came to me with a weave so tangled, there was no choice but to shave it out. Though I didn't want to be the one to turn her into Helen Slater from *The Legend of Billie Jean,* I was the only one she trusted to do it. Candice needed me just like Kristen had. She entrusted me with her vanity, her reputation, and her pride. I couldn't let her down.

Trying to be the best friend I could be and before she could get out the words "nevermind this is a terrible idea," I cocked back my fist and slugged Candice in the face.

Still numb, she darted to the mirror and examined her rapidly swelling eye. Now not only did she look like she was recently Botoxed, but she also looked like she was mugged and possibly raped by a small doctor with no upper body strength.

"This better bruise!" she said like an MMA fighter hoping for a few vanity wounds.

Horrified by my behavior and shocked by how the day had already unraveled, the only thing I could say was, "The first rule of Botox club is, we don't talk about Botox club."

Candice erupted into laughter, then shrieked in pain and ambled to the kitchen for ice. After physically assaulting my good friend, I needed to go home and call my therapist.

"Wait, I probably shouldn't use the ice if I want it to stay blue." Candice held a bag of frozen peas in her hand as I hugged her to leave.

"Use the peas," I urged her.

Later that evening, Jason got a phone call from his good friend Nick, Candice's husband. I was too nervous to eavesdrop, so I threw the dogs in the shower and busied myself with washing them. After a few minutes, there was a knock at the bathroom door. When Jason walked in, his face was grave.

"I just got off the phone with Nick."

Knowing that the best defense was a good offense, I pretended to be annoyed before he could. "Babe, I can't hear you with the water and I have wet dogs in here! Can this wait?"

Jason walked over to the shower and opened the glass door cautiously. "Sorry, honey. I guess Candice's trainer dropped the bench press bar on her face today at the gym. They're canceling dinner this weekend because she has a black eye." He looked at me sweetly, hoping I wasn't disappointed.

"Wow! That's crazy." I exhaled, relieved.

"Why don't you look upset?"

"No, I am! Baby, that's just my face," I reassured him. "I knew I didn't need any more Botox," I said to the dogs under my breath, mentally flipping Sorenson the bird.

Once Jason was fast asleep, I texted Candice to congratulate her on pulling off what I'm sure was the most elaborate hoax of her life and also apologize if I in any way railroaded her into doing something she didn't want to do. I made sure to say all the things I'd failed to tell her before—that she looked amazing for her age, that her effortlessness made her the envy of all her friends, and that she would always be a natural beauty.

I sat there for several minutes, moved by my own words, when my phone lit up with her response.

"What do you think I'd look like with my tits done?"

13.

You Were Molested

Having a sister is like having a best friend who hates you. She shares your parents, shares your clothes, shares your secrets (with her entire circle of friends), and secretly wishes you were twins so that she could have absorbed you in the womb.

My sister and I were born sixteen months apart, and from the earliest time I can remember, we have struggled to differentiate ourselves. This often proved difficult when my mom was busy giving us the exact same middle name or having my sister's tooth pulled so we could be in braces together. Of course, all of it had less to do with my mom's wanting us to be connected and more to do with what was convenient for her. But as a result, Amanda and I have always harbored a small, misguided resentment toward each other that is obviously my mom's fault.

In grade school, I carved out a space for myself as the "overachieving people-pleaser," leaving Amanda no choice but to become the "hot-tempered rebel without a cause." I won the science fair with my herbal Prozac for dogs, while she got suspended for trying to burn down the science room.

As adults, our roles reversed. Amanda joined the workforce and became the responsible, tightly wound sister who sends thank-you cards. And I married an actor.

I guess I shouldn't have expected the best practical joke

I've ever played on someone *ever* to be well received by a girl who is offended by use of the word "panties." But as an older sister, I still felt it my duty to push the envelope.

Shortly after Amanda and Larry started dating, they moved in together. I wasn't seeing a lot of either of them, because I still wasn't comfortable watching them touch. Up until five months ago, Larry had been Jason's newly single friend—up for anything and a complete joy to be around. Now, he was the puppy-lover to my neurotic sister, who wouldn't shut up about whether or not her hips looked wide in her college graduation video from eight years ago.

One night, after a two-hour phone call about her hips, I hung up and packed a bowl. My sister-in-law, Veronica, was in town for the summer, and she and Jason were already three bong hits ahead of me. I walked into the guest bedroom to find the place littered with Twix bars as they swung around on my stripper pole.

"Jenny is the most uncoordinated stripper I've ever seen!" Jason said as he hung from the pole in an upside-down arabesque.

My husband has always been more of my wife, so the fact that he was a better stripper than me was annoying but not a huge surprise.

Just as my high started to take effect, I wobbled toward the stereo and adjusted the volume on the *Twilight* soundtrack.

"Do you find it at all weird that your husband strips?" Veronica asked, tossing a dollar at Jason to reward him for his performance.

"She just hates that I'm better than her!" Jason arrogantly slid down the pole and cat-crawled over to the bong. "Sorry, honey, but you are a horrible mess of a stripper, and I could obviously win *Dancing with the Stars*. . . . Should we order a pizza?"

I was stoned but still felt Jason's cockiness needed a little curbing. I knew he was better, but to let him know he was better would go against all my principles as a woman. I decided the quickest fix would be to bring out his yearbook and remind him that he was on the tennis team and totally married out of his league. Veronica ordered eight pizzas for the three of us while I left to track it down.

After thirty minutes of standing in the garage, trying to remember why I left the house in only a workout bra and boxer shorts, I homed in on a bin of old albums. Opening it, I realized they were mine. Earlier that year, my mom had given my sister and me all our childhood photos as gifts. (Code for: she had no use for them in her new condo.)

Distracted by my own cuteness, I forgot about Jason's yearbook entirely and carried the ten-pound bin back into the house to go through it. The alarming thing about those albums wasn't seeing my parents married and happy (though that was weird too)—but the obvious absence of my sister. There were no shots of her anywhere. I felt like Marty McFly in *Back to the Future,* though I was entirely too high to make it to the Enchantment Under the Sea dance in time to effect any real change. Still, from the look of these pictures, Amanda hadn't ever existed within our family.

I called my mom to make sure I hadn't accidentally smoked mushrooms.

"Mom, remember Amanda? You know, my sister? Why are there no pictures of her in this photo bin?"

"Jenny?" she asked, confused, as if she had had a litter of children and was trying to remember which one I was. "Oh, the baby photos! I separated them. Your sister has all the pics of her and you have all the pics of you."

"So there were no pics of us *together*?"

"I think I threw those out."

Before I could respond, the pizza guy was at the door. I told my mom I'd call her back, which I had no intention of doing, and paid for the pies.

Jason and Veronica floated into the room like Shaggy and Scooby-Doo and immediately started bingeing. Hell-bent on finding evidence of the childhood I was vaguely sure I'd experienced, I continued searching through the photos.

Eventually, I stumbled upon a small four-by-six of Amanda sitting in a rocking chair with our Great-Grandpa Norm. He seemed serene, while Amanda looked scared to death. I guess it made sense: Grandpa Norm was a molester.

Well, to be fair, I'm not certain Grandpa Norm ever really molested anybody. But his brother Mervin did.

As children, we always heard the stories of weird Great-Uncle Mervin from Alabama who went to jail for inappropriate behavior with his children and grandchildren. Details were never expounded upon, because this was the WASPy side of my family—the side that didn't like to suffer through things like "facts" or "reality." Suffice it to say, he was a scary fucking Molester Man.

For as long as I knew him, my Grandpa Norm had no teeth and whenever he kissed you, your mouth would inevitably collapse into his. I never saw him wear anything but overalls, and his welder's hands were swollen from years of hard labor (and probably molesting). He never tried anything on me, but he had this vibe that made you feel like he might be undressing you with his creepy grandpa eyes. His daughter, my Grandma Gayle, was the kind of perennial child who at fifty-five still referred to her breasts as her "privates." She spent most of her adult life hibernating in her house, collecting *Reader's Digests,* and getting drunk on Listerine. Norm's late wife, my

Great-Grandma Jean, carried a revolver in her kitchen apron and slept between Amanda and me every time we spent the night at their house. For this reason, I was certain of two things:

1. Grandpa Norm was a molester (because why else would she insist on sleeping in our bed?), and
2. Amanda and I could *never* have been molested by Grandpa Norm (because we never had any alone time).

Over the years, especially after Grandpa Norm passed, Amanda and I would try to bait my mom into admitting that Grandpa Norm stole her virginity. This was a recurring joke of ours. We were insistent: Her string of weird relationships and her inability to love—they must have been a reaction to a repressed sexual violation by the man she considered her second father. Her response was one of disgust, followed by a lengthy diatribe about how Grandpa Norm was one of the greatest men she'd ever known. We never bought it.

When I walked into the kitchen to share my story, Jason and Veronica were busy discovering the benefits of using a slice of pizza as a plate for another slice of pizza.

I donned my best narrator voice, like Burl Ives in the claymation version of *Rudolph, the Red-Nosed Reindeer* (whom, incidentally, I've also always suspected of being a molester), and told the tale of Grandpa Norm. I explained that my sister and I had been talking about him—with each other, with our mom—for years. I finished my story by pointing out the photo of Amanda on a rocking chair with Grandpa Norm. It was an innocuous snapshot, but it could be the photographic "evidence" I'd long been waiting for. . . .

"I feel like I could have been molested," Veronica said plainly.

"By who?" Jason asked.

"I don't know. Doesn't everyone feel like they might have been molested? Like maybe if I got hypnotized, I'd remember sucking Dad's dick or something." She hopped up on the counter and grabbed another piece of pizza.

"I was never molested, and sometimes it kind of offends me that nobody even tried." I stared at a photo of myself with a hideous bowl cut that I was sure helped dissuade would-be attackers.

"The molestation really helps me understand why your sister is such a cunt," Jason said thoughtfully.

"Jason! She wasn't *really* molested. That was just our running joke. And now I have the perfect photo to support it." I thought for a moment, until inspiration struck.

"Should I send this picture to Amanda with an anonymous note telling her she was molested?"

"Oh my God! That's hilarious," Veronica said, transfixed by her new piece of pizza like she'd spotted an imprint of the Virgin Mary on it.

"I mean, she'll know it's from me, and she obviously knows Grandpa Norm never laid a hand on her, but I still think she'd get a kick out of it."

"You gotta do it. The effort alone is impressive." Veronica could barely contain her excitement.

So for the next two hours, the three of us worked on rough drafts of a letter. Mine read:

Dear Amanda,
I am the woman who took this photo. You were molested.

Love,
A Silent Neighbor

Veronica opted for a more friendly approach:

> Hey Girl,
> Longtime no talk. Hope you're well.
> PS. You were molested. Mall this weekend?

Jason went with the trusty stick figure explanation. He drew two people, with an arrow pointing at each. The first said: "You." The second said: "Me molesting you."

After much debate, I decided my draft sounded the least abrasive. I made Veronica write the note.

"But it's my art!" Jason cried out as he ran back to the stripper pole and did an inverted crucifix.

Ignoring him, Veronica and I folded the photo and letter into the envelope, sealed it, and drove to the nearest mailbox. Under the blanket of night, the letter was sent and subsequently forgotten.

Two days later, I was with Veronica in Century City, having lunch. My phone was on vibrate, but I could feel it going ballistic in my purse. I picked it up and heard Amanda on the other end.

"Jenny! Oh my god! Are you sitting down?"

I was slow to catch on.

"Did you get a letter in the mail today?" she asked.

Grabbing Veronica's thigh, I started to breathe quickly. "No . . . Why?"

"I walked out to get the mail this morning and I opened this cute little envelope I thought was a thank-you note, and guess what it said? It said I was molested by Grandpa Norm!"

I had to cover the phone with my hand as I doubled over

in my seat in anxious hysterics. Pulling myself together, I reengaged. "Well . . . were you?" I asked.

"I don't even know anymore! I called Mom and she had no idea what I was talking about. But this does explain a lot. My need for control, my aversion to anal sex—"

As Amanda continued to spin out her theories, I found myself feeling guiltier and guiltier. I kept waiting for her to mention our ongoing joke about Grandpa Norm, or how she obviously knew the note was a prank. But she remained flummoxed and distraught.

Veronica cleared her throat and motioned for me to hand her the phone.

"Amanda, Veronica wants to talk to you," I said.

I could hear my sister explaining to Veronica how, after opening the letter, she popped two Xanax, called my mom, and then the police. The note was turned over for analysis, and she hoped to know more about the sender later in the week.

"Is it really important who sent it?" Veronica asked.

"I need to know the truth! And the woman who took the photo claims to have answers!" She was yelling now.

I pulled the phone back from Veronica, who kept her head pressed against mine in order to better eavesdrop.

"Listen, Mand, I have to tell you something—"

"Were you molested too?" she sniveled.

"No," I said in my most self-pitying tone.

"I guess I was always the smaller one. More vulnerable, better hair . . ." She trailed off, pleased that someone had chosen her over me.

"Amanda," I tried again.

"Jenny, you probably don't understand this because you aren't a survivor, but I need to worry about myself right now. And my *self* was molested." She was doing her first AA "share" now.

She talked for a few more minutes about the difference between a good touch and a bad touch before I interrupted. My irritation over her narcissism finally outweighed my shame.

"Amanda, I sent the letter."

The phone went silent for several seconds before I felt awkward enough to keep talking.

"We've always had that inside joke about Grandpa Norm being a molester," I said. "I thought you'd think it was funny."

"We don't have any inside joke about Grandpa Norm being a molester," she said, seething.

Overhearing this, Veronica pulled away. "You didn't have an inside joke?" she whispered. She looked at me like I'd just driven a truck over a box of kittens.

"Amanda, we *totally* had that inside joke about Grandpa Norm. Remember, his weird toothless mouth kisses?"

The line went dead.

I spent the next two weeks being sent directly to her voice mail. I had my mom call and remind Amanda that, yes, on occasion we joked about Grandpa Norm molesting people. But like molestation itself, Amanda claimed to have repressed the memory. She was furious I'd duped her in such a dark way and insisted Jason donate money to Childhelp as penance. Later we heard about her police report. Apparently, it was summed up something like: "No silent neighbor, just a mentally ill sister."

A month passed, and Amanda and Larry finally agreed to come over for dinner. Halfway through dessert, Amanda grabbed her head like she was experiencing a posttraumatic stress flashback.

"Who does that?" she vented. "I mean, I knew you were sick, but I never thought you were *that* sick!" I could tell Larry wanted to laugh, but Amanda would have cut his balls off and fed them to him if he had.

"Would it have been less offensive if we'd used stick figures?" Jason asked. "For the record, I wanted to send stick figures."

"Amanda, I'm the only person in the world who'd have access to your baby photos. Including our own mother. I thought you'd put it together." I tried to plead my case, but Amanda wouldn't budge.

The worst part was that every time she tried explaining how "unfunny" it was, Jason and I couldn't help bursting into laughter. The whole thing sounded so ridiculous, and hearing it again, as told by Amanda, only seemed to make it funnier.

In retrospect, I guess I should have been more sensitive. But being sensitive is *her* job! I'm the fun, outgoing sister who sends molestation letters! It's just the role I've assumed. What I really learned from this event was that not everyone appreciates my comic genius. Even though Amanda and I grew up with similar life experiences, we are very different people. She's not hot enough to be molested and I totally am.

14.

Everyone Wants to Kill Me

For as long as I can remember, I've always felt like everyone was out to kill me. And not like accidentally nab me with a stray bullet during an L.A. riot, but more like consciously abduct me, rape me, keep me in a box, only feed me products made with high-fructose corn syrup, and eventually turn me into a skin tuxedo. When I was a child, it made sense to carry Mace and a staple gun in my backpack in case I needed to fight off a child molester. But as an adult, my extreme paranoia has gotten me into more trouble than out of it.

I was raised by a single mom who, for the majority of my childhood, was on a date while my sister and I ordered happy hour fish tacos in a booth on the opposite side of the bar. From an early age we were warned by her of the pitfalls that came with being "absolutely adorable creatures who look just like their mother." She reasoned that, as her offspring, we were clearly the two most attractive children alive, and therefore also the ultimate child-abducting murderer conquests. We grew up knowing to sound the alarm if anyone ever offered us candy, asked to drive us home from school, or showed up at the front door claiming to be Jehovah's Witnesses. She'd tell us about little girls who weren't half as attractive as we were getting stolen on their walks home from school and driven across the border from San Diego into Mexico to become sex slaves. We had a code word to signify distress ("forest") and questions to ask if someone tried to claim they were a family friend. (What tattoo does my mom have on her butt? Answer: an Aztec sun, motherfucker! Anyone who really knew my mom knew how important her butt tattoo was to her. One of her musician boyfriends even wrote a song about it called "Lady with the Fireball Bottom.") In fairness, I think my mom was trying to instill a sense of street smarts into Amanda and me. Instead, she made us into people who need sedatives to go to the dog park.

The real problem was that nobody was ever looking after us. Between work and dating, both our baby-booming parents were preoccupied with their own lives. As a result, Amanda and I were forced to look after ourselves, armed with the knowledge that mortal danger could lurk around any and all corners. The world is a scary place when you are young and on your own. Everyone is a potential predator, everything is a potential trap, and nowhere feels completely safe. That "bottom could fall out at any moment" mentality is how I live my life.

When I reached middle school, my fears about being abducted took a supernatural turn. I accidentally saw the trailer for a movie called *Fire in the Sky*. The film is based on the real-life account of a guy named Travis Walton who claimed he was abducted by aliens in the Arizona desert while working as a logger in 1975. Instantly, "alien abduction" topped the list of ways I might be killed. Even though Scottsdale, a suburb of Phoenix, seemed a little conspicuous for a spaceship sighting, I felt my compassionate understanding of other cultures and my near telepathic relationship with animals probably made it worthwhile for the aliens to take some risks. Before bed, I ritualistically checked all the doors in the house to make sure they were locked. Then I tied my blinds to the base of a nearby chair in a booby trap–like knot. Through extensive research, I'd learned that aliens preferred attacking from the inside out. Meaning: mind control. The loose rigging on the blinds wasn't intended to stop the aliens from coming in; it was intended to stop me from going out. If they got inside my head, I'd be in a trancelike state and under their control. I needed something in the room to get tangled in, to startle me out of my hypnosis, and to remind me that I'm not emotionally strong enough to live in an intergalactic prison.

In high school, I gave up on waiting for my alien abduction and decided to focus my energy on malicious ghosts. When I'd visit California, I imagined they were the disgruntled spirits of eighteenth-century Spanish missionaries who felt my mom was cock-teasing her gardener. In Arizona, I assumed my house was built on a sacred Indian burial ground whose former inhabitants were offended by my dad's flagrant misuse of the color turquoise. I could never stand in the bathroom with the lights off. I could never sleep with my closet door open. And I could *never* look in a mirror in my bedroom after midnight. I wasn't really sure what a ghost could even do to hurt me; I just felt like actually seeing one would lead to my demise.

By college, I reverted back to the classic "rapist in a windowless van" paranoia. My therapist would often tell me that it was incredibly narcissistic of me to assume something so horrific and unusual would happen to me, but I figured she just didn't know me well enough yet to realize how awesome I was. Also, she might just have been trying to get me to drop my guard in order to lure me into the basement of her building, where she likely kidnapped and kept her other attractive female patients chained to hospital beds in order to harvest their ovaries.

Once out of college and truly on my own, I practiced being a tough bitch to any and all nefarious-looking individuals.

EXT. BUSY LOS ANGELES STREET CORNER – DAY

A clean-cut, nice-looking STRANGER pulls up to JENNY in his car.

Stranger
Hey, do you know how I get to Sunset Boulevard?

Jenny backs away as she talks.

Jenny
No! I don't live here.

Stranger
But . . .

Jenny
I said no! Get the fuck away from me! Fire!!!

Jenny runs off in the opposite direction.

Without the distractions of school or a job, I had time to grow skeptical of other, more commonplace scenarios. I decided that I couldn't do road trips through small towns, because at night the townspeople would obviously turn into *Deliverance*-esque hillbillies and butcher me. I couldn't ride in taxis alone without being on the phone, because if I hung up, the driver would turn into *The Bone Collector* and, again, butcher me. I couldn't valet my car, because when the vehicle was out of sight, a really limber carjacker would pretzel himself into my backseat (butchering optional). And I couldn't travel to Florida, because a cop might pull me over on a deserted road in the middle of the night and sodomize me, then shoot himself in the leg and put my fingerprints on the gun. There were myriad death traps waiting for me right outside my front door. So I decided to play it safe by staying inside and becoming anorexic.

While I worried about homicidal maniacs, Amanda became a hypochondriac. Our phone calls usually went something like this:

"Hey," I'd say.

"Hey."

"I think the guy in the apartment next to me just said 'bless you' when I sneezed. Do you think he installed cameras in here when I was out, or do you think he's drilled a peephole?"

"I think I have a blood clot. You should come over this weekend and pick out what things of mine you'd want in the event that I don't make it." Amanda would clear her throat dramatically. "Also, I think your apartment just has really thin walls. Has your super ever checked for asbestos?"

Amanda didn't die that weekend, nor the weekend after that. And with age and Valium, her paranoia lessened. Mine, however, did not.

Jason moved to Atlanta for the summer to shoot a movie. He was to be gone for three months, the longest he'd been away our entire marriage. On previous occasions, I'd usually find replacement husbands to stay in the house and protect me. For the film in Seattle, it was my recently divorced acting coach and his six-year-old son, who ended up calling me Mommy and tried to light Teets on fire. For the press trip to Brazil, it was my trainer, his girlfriend, and their mini fridge filled with HGH. But this time, it was my sister-in-law Veronica.

Being a teacher, Veronica's entire identity and sense of motivation crumbles as soon as it hits June. All she wants to do at the end of a school year is sit in darkness and eat diet pills and premade frosting. It had become tradition for her to fly out to L.A. in her cupcake-printed pajama pants and skulk around our house ambitionless until eventually it was August. Over the years, she'd become a mildly depressed fixture on our couch and a symbol of summer.

For Jason's going-away dinner, we took Veronica out with my then-pregnant sister, Amanda, and her husband, Larry. Larry had a buddy who'd just opened a new gastropub downtown and insisted we try it. The tasting menu had everything—foie gras lollipops, burrata and uni salads, piles of *Ibérico* ham, and deconstructed mashed potatoes. I couldn't eat much, because my nerves were already acting up. I knew in my gut I wasn't going to feel safe with just Veronica in the house. Any murderer worth his salt would take one look at Veronica and realize she already hated her life and that there would be no point in killing her.

"So, you freaking out about Jason going?" Amanda stuffed a handful of ham into her face.

"She's gonna be fine. Besides, Vern is staying there for at least the first half," Jason said.

"Wait! What? Only the first half?" This was the first I was hearing that my five-foot-tall guardian who sleeps till 3 P.M. was in fact planning on abandoning me halfway through Jason's time away.

"I got a babysitting gig. Gotta go home early this year. This is the best prosciutto I've ever had." Veronica chomped on her ham and shrugged.

"It's not prosciutto! Prosciutto is Italian. This is from Spain. It's called *Ibérico.* It's special because these pigs were raised on only acorns. It gives the meat a distinctly nutty flavor," Jason explained.

"I . . . I mean, I'm gonna have to check into a hotel or something." I was starting to panic.

"We have a security system—and dogs, Jen. You'll be fine. I want to buy some of this stuff. Don't you think we should? It's excellent."

Larry and Jason took tours of the kitchen after dinner, and both placed orders for their own individual *Ibérico* legs. Amanda, meanwhile, sensing my desperation, warned me that she was turning her guest bedroom into a nursery at the end of the month, so not to get any ideas about crashing with her once Veronica left town.

My house is precariously perched on the side of a mountain. I can't tell you which mountain, because I wouldn't want to tempt you into murdering me. But let's just say that I don't have many neighbors, and the ones I do have are rarely in town. Originally, the guy next door was an eccentric gay porn star named Xian, who traveled back and forth to Asia for work. He was a collector of exotic birds and large cats, all of which I'm certain were on the endangered species list. One time while we were out of town, our maid called, saying that a baby mountain lion was sitting on our bed, wearing a Goyard collar. (She knows what Goyard is because I bought her a knockoff downtown for her birthday.) The animal turned out to be a Savannah cat named Ingrid, who escaped again months later and committed suicide on Sunset Boulevard. After Ingrid's untimely death, Xian moved out, leaving the house vacant and on the market for over a year. During that time, I became convinced that a Satanic cult was squatting inside after I swore I heard someone screaming "Let Jesus fuck you!" from the gazebo one night.

Across the shared driveway was the wild child Olympic gold medalist, Tyler Black. When Tyler moved in, I felt old, unattractive, and unaccomplished. At just twenty-five, he'd won three Olympics, had his own video game, his own clothing line, hosted *The View,* did a movie with Scorsese, dated Gisele Bündchen, and drove four different Maseratis. I felt safe having Tyler around because he was too preoccupied with his own life to think about killing me, and because he was a more valuable target for psychopaths than I was. Tyler was a prodigy at the height of his success, and the world was his oyster. I was just the nice older woman next door who helped him compose text messages to whatever Victoria's Secret model he was currently fucking. We exchanged house keys in case either of us were ever away for too long and our dogs needed to be let out. When Jason was out of town, Tyler always invited me out with his entourage and could never understand when I'd say no. Though it sometimes felt like living in a frat house when I'd come home to a palm tree arbitrarily thrown in my swimming pool or his life-sized Wheaties box mounted on the dining room table, I enjoyed having the company. Unfortunately, Tyler's training schedule kept him on the road for the majority of the year. And during an Olympic year, his house was all but abandoned (which left room for the Satanic cult to branch out to a second campus). There was just one neighbor left: Mickey Gervich.

Mickey was a small Jewish man of about fifty. He was a successful songwriter from Boston who rarely left his house and was only ever seen walking down the driveway to get his mail in a Bart Simpson shirt that barely covered his ass and a pair of Tevas. Jason and I never had much interaction with

Mickey. Nobody did. His meals and groceries were delivered to the front door like he was a part of Project Angel Food. He didn't know how to drive, so he always used a car service. And he seemed to do most of his work at night (aka "the witching hours"). No matter what time it was, I could always look out my window and see the flickering lights of a television screen shooting through the curtains of his upstairs window. Three years ago, I was in my driveway when a tall Jamaican woman pulled up to his house in a silver Toyota Camry. She'd just moved from Palm Beach and claimed to be Mickey's fiancée. After several weeks, I never saw her again. Even if the rest of the neighbors were away, I knew Mickey would always be home. But since he was a five-foot-two agoraphobic, I didn't really know what Mickey was going to be able to do to protect me.

Living with Veronica felt like living with an old lady who needed to go to a retirement home but didn't have any kids around to force her. Her favorite thing to do was sit in front of the TV with a mug of overly sweetened coffee and think she was solving crime shows. This was the summer of the Casey Anthony trial and coverage of her daughter's gruesome death was inescapable. In between updates on the young mother's murder trial, Veronica would tune in to other equally disconcerting programs like *Unsolved Mysteries, Dateline,* and the eleven o'clock news. For a neurotic mess like me, Veronica was possibly the worst houseguest I could have. But despite my desire to tame my inner scaredy-cat, I couldn't help but want to know every last detail about any and all psychotic events going on in the world. I needed to stay one step ahead of my murderer and know the latest kidnapping and murder trends. And the only way to do that was to study the missteps of others.

After a few weeks of Nancy Grace pointing out how just because someone looks innocent doesn't mean they are, I started to reevaluate the peripheral characters in my life. My suspicions immediately fell on Mickey.

"My neighbor, Mickey Gervich, was engaged to a Zanida Gonzales," I said to Veronica one night while peering out the window, deep in thought. "Maybe that wasn't her name. But I think it was something like that. I only met her once. Then she mysteriously vanished. Do you think he killed her?"

"How do you live in the world?" Unfazed by my paranoia, she continued reading her new favorite book, *A Stolen Life* by Jaycee Dugard.

Between Tyler and Xian, I had never taken the time to focus on Mickey. He kept to himself. And as HLN pointed out, people who keep to themselves usually have crawl spaces filled with skulls. It was all coming together now. I kicked myself for my naïveté. A killer had been right under my nose all the time, just like a shitty episode of *Murder, She Wrote.*

"How does one miss a six-foot-tall Jamaican chick? Where did she go? Six-foot-tall Jamaicans don't just disappear," I said, inadvertently adopting a slight New England accent à la Jessica Fletcher.

"This was three years ago? They probably broke up." Engrossed in the case, Veronica gnawed at her cuticles until they started bleeding. "This chick is so guilty."

"Or she's in his basement!" I looked over to Nancy Grace, who stared back at me from inside the TV. I could tell she agreed with me.

"Are you still talking about your neighbor? Get off it!" Veronica blotted her hands on the oversized hoodie she'd had on since arriving at our house three weeks ago.

"There's a great *Dateline* on tonight, but I'm not gonna let you watch it if you're gonna make me sleep in bed with you again."

"What's it about?" I wanted to be uninterested, but I couldn't help myself.

"A neighbor who kills someone."

That night, Keith Morrison (who couldn't possibly look more like a serial killer himself) narrated a story about a married couple who bought a house in Big Sur that landed them in a two-year-long dispute with their elderly neighbor over a shared driveway. The story ended in a 911 phone call, where you could hear the elderly man shoot both the husband and wife in the back after a screaming match outside their home.

"Maybe that wasn't the best episode to show you," Veronica said later that night as she turned over in bed to find me and my dogs lying next to her.

As I lay there trying to sleep, all I could think about was Mickey. From the guest bedroom window, I could see the lights in Mickey's house still on. I wondered if he'd just watched the same program. I wondered if he owned any firearms. And I wondered if he knew that I was on to him.

The next day, my neighbor Tyler texted to tell me he'd be back in town for the weekend, and I couldn't have been more relieved. He invited Veronica and me to a vodka party he was hosting at the Chateau Marmont. Veronica wanted to go, but the only outfit she had brought besides her cupcake pajama pants was a black muumuu that made her look like a dirty bar wench from Medieval Times. Desperate to attend the party, Veronica agreed to let Amanda and me take her shopping for more suitable attire.

Amanda arrived at my house around noon, still pregnant. She was in her final month and unable to not look like a giant weather balloon. She floated into the house, fuming.

"It's so damn hot outside, I can't feel my feet. And I'm definitely not driving."

"It's fine. I'll drive," I said, grabbing my keys as a signal to Veronica to stop fucking with her eyeliner and hurry up.

We pulled out of the garage, careful to not hit Amanda's brand-new SUV, expertly parked like an asshole in the center of our shared driveway.

"Are you sure she can just leave her car like that?" Veronica asked.

"What does that mean?" Amanda's face started to turn red with hormones and fury.

"Mickey doesn't drive, and Tyler isn't back till tomorrow." I changed the subject before Amanda could sulk and change her mind about coming with us. "Love the new car, by the way."

"When you're responsible for new life, an SUV is the only way to go. I don't think I'd feel safe in anything else." The baby wasn't even out of her, and she already sounded smug.

At the store, Veronica tried on several different dresses and eventually settled on one that looked identical to the muumuu she had at home. She claimed it was the only thing she felt sexy in. When we got back to the house, somebody was waiting for us beside Amanda's car: Mickey Gervich.

"What the fuck?" I said under my breath.

"What is that little man doing touching my car?" Amanda asked, annoyed.

"That's the guy Jenny thinks is going to kill her," Veronica said casually, barely looking up from her phone.

"He's a tiny Jew. Tiny Jews don't kill. Do they?" Amanda momentarily looked down at her stomach, concerned, then back up at Mickey. "He better not be breaking into my car!"

I parked and approached Mickey slowly.

"Hey, Mickey," I said in a neighborly "don't kill me, there are witnesses around" tone.

"This car was blocking the entire driveway, and my gardeners couldn't get their truck up because of it. I'm having trees pulled today. You weren't home and I didn't recognize the vehicle, so I was going to have it towed." He spoke in a frazzled, pissed-off tone.

Behind me, a tow truck made its way up the hill toward Amanda's car.

"What! No! I'm her sister! I'll move the car! It's brand-new! I'm pregnant!" Amanda opened her car, threw herself in the driver's seat, and locked the doors.

"Sorry, Mickey. I really didn't mean to inconvenience you. I just figured since you're afraid to drive and all, I didn't think you'd need access—"

He cut me off before I could finish. "I'm 'afraid' to drive? That's quite an assumption. I actually don't drive because of my vision. But to be frank, it's really none of your business."

"You're absolutely right. Sorry. Anyway, we'll move the car."

Before I could say anything to Amanda, she was driving away.

Mickey turned and walked back into his house, and Veronica followed me into mine.

"*Fuuuuck!* This isn't happening! Last night's *Dateline* is becoming my real life!" I paced around the house, frantic.

"See, this looks totally different than the other dress." Veronica pulled her new muumuu over her old muumuu and showed me all the subtle differences. "What do you think?"

"I think I just upset the guy who is tops on my list of potential murderers. I *think* we need to move." I looked over at Teets asleep on the couch, still not realizing I was home. It was clear he wasn't going to be of any help if Mickey decided to force his way into the house.

"Okay, yes. He seemed a little pissed, I'm not gonna lie,

but he definitely didn't seem like he was at the point yet where he'd want you dead."

"Yet?"

"Yeah, not yet."

"'Not yet' implies that he eventually will," I cried.

"Jenny, get a hold of yourself. Nothing is happening."

As the sun set over the canyon, Veronica and I sat on the patio drinking tequila, petting my utterly useless guard dogs, and discussing what Jane Velez-Mitchell looked like before her plastic surgeon gave her Michael Jackson's face. I momentarily forgot about Mickey and enjoyed the summer night like a normal person who doesn't feel like their neighbor wants to murder them.

By midnight, all my fears came flooding back. I went to set the house alarm, but for some reason it wasn't working.

"Jesus Christ, he's cut the wires!" I screamed, leaping to the most obvious explanation first.

"Oh God. I shouldn't have let you get buzzed. Now you're really gonna be annoying." Veronica laughed at me and went to wash her face for bed.

She was right, I rarely drank and after half a glass of anything, I could usually be counted on to say or do something I'd regret in the morning.

"I'm serious, Vern! The alarm was working perfectly fine, and now it's not! That only happens when somebody *cuts* the wires. Go check the phone line."

I grabbed my cell and dialed ADT Home Security.

"Yes, hi. My alarm isn't letting me set it, and I think it might have been tampered with," I said.

"The phone lines work, psycho!" Veronica called out from the kitchen.

"Well, ma'am," the operator said, "the soonest we could

get a technician out there to work on it would be two weeks from now."

"Look, I could be dead in two weeks if somebody doesn't come *now*."

"It's past business hours, and we won't be able to accommodate your request until at least—"

I stopped her. "Okay, fine. I need a patrolman to just come to the house and just keep a lookout through the night. . . . Maybe two."

"Armed response is included in your package only when your alarm has been set off," she responded mechanically.

"Well, it's not going to be set off, because someone has obviously fucked with it." I started to hyperventilate. "Okay, fine, I want to up my package. I want the biggest plan you offer. I want soldiers."

Just then, Veronica walked back in and tore the phone from my hands. "Jenny, go get in my bed!"

I drunkenly obliged. That night I dreamt of dozens of soldiers (who coincidentally all looked exactly like Jake Gyllenhaal in *Jarhead*) teeming around my property with machine guns, overturning decorative rocks to expose potential land mines, and snipers on my roof ready to take out Mickey and whoever else might try to enter without permission. I think the actual "soldiers" were two forty-year-old guys in a Prius with an ADT logo who cruised by the house once or twice and spent the rest of the night sitting in their car, watching each other masturbate.

By morning, the threat of Mickey breaking in was gone. I agreed that I'd overreacted and promised to make a concerted effort not to dwell on death for the next twenty-four hours. It was the day of Tyler's party, and we had to prepare. I walked outside and saw three Mercedes sedans already parked in front of his house, letting me know he was home.

Veronica spent the latter half of the afternoon blow-drying her hair and waxing her face. Feeling suddenly self-conscious about the girth of her arms, she asked if I had a long-sleeve camisole she could wear underneath her dress (which was actually a muumuu). When it was time to go, Veronica needed twenty more minutes to look in the mirror, tilting her head and analyzing her look.

When she finally appeared in the living room, she was wearing her black dress, black leggings, a black long-sleeve shirt, and black boots.

"I know it's more of a fall look, but what do you think?"

I thought she looked like a Saudi housewife minus the hijab.

"You look great," I said.

After taking seventeen pictures she didn't approve of, we finally got one she agreed to post online, locked up the house, and left for Chateau Marmont.

Within an hour of arriving, Veronica met an indie drummer and disappeared. I, meanwhile, ate Jell-O shots and wandered around, telling whoever would listen about Mickey.

"Wait, Mickey Gervich? The songwriter? Trust me, you have absolutely nothing to worry about. That guy couldn't hurt you if he tried," said a portly guy who commenced to sit openmouthed under the vodka ice luge. "He's repped by my firm. He's just quirky. Have you seen his purple Tevas?"

"I don't know that I've seen the purple pair," I said, locking eyes with Veronica, who was now sitting on the drummer's lap across the bar.

I excused myself and walked over to her. It had been four hours, and I was more than ready to go home.

"Okay, seriously. I just accidentally brought up the fact that I thought Mickey was a murderer to a guy who actually knows him. I'm so embarrassed. What if that gets back to him? Jason is gonna be furious. He hates when I suspect people we know of being murderers."

"That fat guy under the ice luge? You're fine. He's wasted. I want you to meet Beau."

The drummer stood up and extended his hand. "Right on. Nice to meet you."

He couldn't have been more than twenty-five years old, with shaggy blond hair, an ironic mustache, and jeans that were tighter than Veronica's leggings.

"I think I need to go home. I don't trust that I won't keep talking to the wrong people." I watched Veronica's hand make its way down the drummer's pants.

"I'll get a ride home in a few," she said. "Beau has a suite here, and he's gonna show me around." She licked her lips predatorily.

"Fine. Ring the gate when you get back, and I'll let you in," I said, searching through my purse for my valet stub.

After scanning my car for hijackers, I drove back to my cul-de-sac with increasing anxiety. I tried to calm myself by remembering that Tyler and entourage would be following shortly, and that the fat guy under the luge said Mickey couldn't hurt a fly. As I pulled up to the house, I noticed a large package with a note on it sitting by the front gate. Fumbling with my keys, I picked it up and carried it inside. I threw the heavy package on the table and checked around the room for broken glass. Once I was sure the coast was clear, I pulled the note off the package and read it.

Had this in my fridge all day. Think it's for you guys.
—Mickey

My hand started to shake as I tore into the box. Beneath a thick layer of Styrofoam, I saw packets of dry ice cradling what looked like . . . preserved flesh. Before inspecting any further, I ran upstairs to the bedroom and locked myself inside. I left my dogs in the living room as an offering and frantically called Veronica's cell. The call went straight to voice mail so I hung up and dialed again. Before her phone could start ringing, I heard a noise coming from the front entrance. The dogs rose to the occasion and started barking as the door pushed back and forth. Then, suddenly, I heard it open.

I'd gone through what I'd do in the event of a home invasion over a million times in my head. My plan was to always grab the thickest blanket I could find and wrap myself in it as I jumped off my balcony into the trees and hoped they were strong enough to catch me. Then, I'd scurry down the branches, suffering a few minor cuts and scrapes along the way, and run barefoot to a nearby neighbor. (Preferably not one who was trying to kill me.)

When I actually thought my home was being invaded, I unfortunately did what all idiot virgins do in every horror movie ever made. I unlocked my bedroom door and stood at the top of the stairs unarmed.

"Hello?"

"It's me! And Beau!" Veronica called out. "Sorry, I didn't ring the bell. Tyler gave me his key. Beau's bandmate had a chick in their room, so we're just gonna bone here."

Traumatized, I slowly made my way down the stairs. Veronica flipped on the lights and offered Beau a drink.

"Oh, look! Jason's *Ibérico* came! When did this get here?" Veronica opened up the rest of the package and pulled out a shrink-wrapped leg of cured ham.

"It . . . I . . . I guess they delivered it to Mickey's house by accident."

"What, you didn't think it was, like, a dead body or something, did you?" Veronica chased Beau around the kitchen, laughing. "She's scared of the neighbor and everyone."

"You don't think I'm a killer, do you?" Beau joked as Veronica led him into the guest bedroom.

"Wait, you're not weird about blood or anything, are you? Because I think I just started my period." She slammed the bedroom door shut behind them.

A month and a half later, Casey Anthony was found innocent, my sister had her baby, I moved out of her nursery, and Jason came home. Before Veronica left for Jersey, she polished off what was left of the *Ibérico*. Beau never called her after that night, which she said was fine because his dick felt like a tampon.

With Jason back in town, I stopped watching the kind of TV that kept me up at night. Much like my liquor, I learned that I just couldn't "hold" my crime shows. And Jason preferred watching *The Bachelor* anyway.

Eventually he ordered another leg of meat and had Larry and Amanda over to share it. I was in the kitchen, eating a pastry out of the trash—one I'd tried to protect myself from earlier by covering in salt and smashing up in a napkin—when Jason walked in from outside.

"Jenny . . ."

"I know what this looks like, but I decided it was worth the calories and unfortunately I had to do a little Dumpster diving to salvage it—"

"Just ran into Mickey in the driveway."

"Oh?" I said innocently.

"Yeah, he was a little confused as to why you've been telling people he's a murderer."

"Oh?" I said again in the exact same voice.

Jason took the pastry out of my hand and bit into it. "You know, I'd almost feel bad for the guy who tried to murder you. Especially if he thought he was gonna keep you alive for a few days in his basement or something. Oy god, that'd be exhausting."

His words sank in, and they gave me a bit of newfound confidence. Maybe I was a murderer's worst nightmare. Maybe my neuroses, childhood defenses I'd always tried to hide, were in fact my greatest weapon against lunatics as an adult. After all, there's got to be nothing more frustrating to a psychopath than being in the company of an equally crazy person who's stealing your thunder. From that day forward, I decided I wasn't going to get hijacked, raped, maimed, or abducted. I was going to die the way other, happy, well-adjusted people with a positive outlook on life did: cancer.

15.

The Bloody Truth About Hollywood

As an actor, you spend your life in Hollywood playing the lottery and hoping to hear your number called. You do the one-off guest appearances you hope will make a splash all over the USA Network. You make out with Steve Carell for a few days in an attempt to steal the scene in a movie nobody except your agent will ever know you were in. (Guys, I was in a movie with Steve Carell.) You fight tooth and nail to be viewed as a comedic actress, a dramatic actress, a young actress, a black actress, or a toothless mother of six with a meth problem who can speak to ghosts. You ride the vicissitudes of fortune because you're steadfast in the belief that someday, someone is bound to take notice. Well, kids, here's the hard truth: Most of you will never be noticed, not by your industry, not by your community, and most definitely not by your parents.

Here are four mistakes my family made that led to me getting headshots and auditioning for a living. Hopefully you can learn from them and not make these mistakes with your own children.

1. Do Not Send Your Child to a Performing Arts Camp

Performing arts camp is designed to build false confidence in children who don't need it.

I was in middle school when my dad sent me to a theater camp for the summer. There, I was cast as the lead in *The Sound of Music,* a role I didn't even compete for. I was blond and the rest of the girls in my class were brunettes, so I was the obvious choice for Maria. I was also the only one who could stand in front of a group of strangers without peeing or eating my hair. We performed only three numbers from the show, but that didn't stop me from telling everyone who would listen that I was in a summer stock production of the Rodgers and Hammerstein classic. I watched endless footage of Julie Andrews to help me prepare. I chased my sister around the house like she was a Von Trapp child and would say things like, "When the Lord closes a door, somewhere he opens a window." That line was cut from our production because it sounded too religious, but I decided the sentiment would be my character's hidden secret. According to our director, actors often pick a secret their character has that they never share with anyone else in the play. That phrase would be mine. And if you by chance caught my performance at the Scottsdale Center for the Performing Arts in 1992, you probably already intuited that. Overnight, I fancied myself an artist. I took a long, drawn-out bow at curtain call and noticed my dad in the sixth row actually looking at me instead of at his endless stacks of paperwork. When I was onstage, my parents—who otherwise couldn't care less about my extracurricular activities—were forced to sit in complete darkness and focus on *only me.* Unlike the other children in my company, who used the stage as a way to overcome their social anxieties, I used it as a way to extract love (or at least an obligatory catcall) out of my parents.

2. Don't Ignore Your Children

If you want to spend your life focused on yourself, great! Don't have kids. If you have kids, however, try to at least pretend to be interested in them. Otherwise, those kids are going to become damaged actors who eventually show their genitals for money. When I got back to school after my summer of love and adoration, I could easily have continued with my previously planned, mainstream pursuit of becoming a marine biologist and followed a career that would have earned me some legitimate respect. Unfortunately, my life went back to normal, my parents went back to focusing on themselves, and I ditched my dreams of becoming the first marine biologist to ride a killer whale from San Diego harbor to the Gulf of Mexico. Now, however, I had a hole in my heart that, before it was filled with applause and roses, I had no idea existed. I had had a taste of what my father's approval looked like, and I yearned for more. My mom wasn't interested in whether I was onstage or not, but fuck her. There was a whole world of moms out there just waiting to hear me sing "Do-Re-Mi."

3. Avoid Taking Your Kid to See *Phantom of the Opera*

Even if your kid doesn't become an actor, he can still turn into one of those weird theater techie geeks who wears a *Phantom* shirt every day of high school and never gets laid. You don't want this for your child. You also don't want your kid to learn all the lyrics to *Phantom*. Once this occurs, he's crossed the Rubicon. Knowing all the lyrics to *Phantom* leads to knowing all the lyrics to *Les Mis,* and knowing all the lyrics to *Les Mis* means your kid is officially on his way to becoming *a thespian*.

I had to take three years of high school drama before I was offered the right to join the International Thespian Society. The ITS was essentially the high school drama club, except that it was recognized around the world and they gave you a button. I was finally part of an international community of artists, and I couldn't have been happier. Once in, I was invited to miming seminars, fringe festivals, and the weird goth guy from the yogurt shop's drunk driving arraignment. I'd fallen into a world of overly loud, overly dramatic outcasts who all got their septums pierced at Hot Topic. All of us planned to audition for college theater programs. For some, the dream was to eventually be the Phantom on Broadway. For those who knew the limitations of their vocal abilities, it was to become Meryl Streep.

4. Do Not Let Your Kid Major in Theater

If your kid majors in theater in college, he or she will believe that they are going to be famous. And they're not. You are also further validating their self-importance and feeding into the fantasy that their degree will actually translate into a real-world job. The only real-world job I can think of where what I learned in college might come in handy is "birthday party princess" or "Elvis impersonator." When you break it down, theater school is really just drama history, vocal exercises, and girls having abortions.

My parents let me major in theater because I told them that feast or famine, acting was what I wanted to do with my life.

"I didn't choose this, it chose me." I tried to explain to my mere mortal family members that my path was preordained and that I had no choice but to embrace my destiny.

I prepared two contrasting monologues and sixteen bars of a song for my series of school auditions. I flew to NYC, Boston, and finally Los Angeles, eager to win the hearts of drama professors everywhere with my epic interpretation of Abigail Williams from *The Crucible*. For my second monologue, I chose *Butterflies Are Free*. I also had a *Twelfth Night* up my sleeve, in the event that they wanted something period. I waited in line at each audition, knowing I was the find of the season. What the other hopefuls surrounding me didn't realize (because I was an actor and hid it so well) was that I'd just come off a successful two-weekend run as Adelaide in *Guys and Dolls* at my high school. That's right, the best role in the whole goddamn show! I was a leading lady standing in a sea of singing trees and I was ready for my close up.

I got into all but one of the programs I applied to and kept my one rejection letter to frame and one day display next to my Oscar. I chose UCLA because I felt being in Los Angeles strengthened my odds of being discovered while still in school. After announcing to my graduating class that I was off to follow my dreams, I bought a copy of Uta Hagen's *Respect for Acting* and focused only on respecting acting while I waited for my big break.

Guess what, kids? My big break never came. I got out of school, and reality smacked me across the face. Now, instead of just a handful of playful peers, I was competing against professionals who'd been working in film and TV since before I'd even heard of theater camp. I wasn't the gifted actress that years of conditioning and coddling led me to believe. I was pretty much a total amateur hack who had no idea what I was doing. I didn't know how to audition without looking directly into the camera. I was broad and over the top with an inability to stand still. I was afraid to be funny because I didn't want to seem like a bimbo, and I was always too loud because I still thought I needed to project. In my mind, I thought I was doing great work. I considered myself a dramatic tour de force and turned even Taco Bell auditions into crying scenes where I'd have an entire nervous breakdown. I'd walk into a room and immediately start mentioning all the places I'd studied, then say things like, "This episode of *Law and Order* truly feels like it follows all the rules of a great Aristotilean tragedy." When I'd get a callback, I assumed I basically had the job. Then when I didn't get the job, I'd beat myself up and fall into a deep depression. I hung Goethe quotes on my walls (*"I wish the stage were as narrow as the wire of a tightrope dancer, so that no incompetent would dare step upon it."*) and wrote in my journal about how one day I would emerge like a phoenix from the ashes. I tried to build myself back up by thinking about how I'd answer James Lipton's Proust Questionaire and taking new headshots where I wore a simple turtleneck and stared at the camera expressionless. I was serious and needed Hollywood to know it.

My dad continued to pay my rent while I insisted fame and fortune were just around the corner. If I were I boy, I feel like he would have forced me to get a job, but since I was a girl, I don't think he expected my contribution to society to be great anyway. Eventually, I learned how to audition, but it took years to learn how to actually work and even longer to make any money at it. With perseverance and the right boyfriends, I finally found my footing.

By my mid-twenties, I'd lost my entitled drama-school-cunt attitude, stopped referring to myself as "Baby Judi Dench," and started doing television guest stars. I played the girlfriend, the grieving witness, the hard-hitting FBI investigator, the zombie-fighting teenager, the privileged trophy wife, the desperate chick at the office, and the girl who got raped by Tom Sizemore. Sometimes I'd recur for a whole season; other times I'd get Tasered to death by Patricia Arquette within the first thirty minutes of an episode. I shot a handful of independent films and even the occasional commercial, but nothing seemed to pop. I was always the random girl from that random thing you caught showing her jugs on Starz at 3 A.M.

So why did I keep going? The same reason all actors do—because there is always the promise of that dream job just around the corner. Actors are like gamblers. We can't help but think that if we cash in our chips and walk away, some other bitch is going to be buying Chanel boots with our jackpot. We are addicts and we want our Chanel boots!

Over the course of my career, I've come to consider myself one of the most "almost-hired" actresses in the game. I've been inches away from jobs that could have changed the course of my life, and watched them slip through my fingers, sometimes for the most arbitrary reasons. Just like a roulette wheel, Hollywood is random. But the closer you get to almost hearing your number called, the deeper into your pockets you dig. And I've dug and dug and basically bet my entire self-worth on winning something substantial. When you are up, there is nothing like it. But when you are down, your life feels meaningless. For the 2 percent of the time you feel like Angelina Jolie, there's that other 98 percent where you feel like her creepy brother, James Haven.

While in college I wrote a one-woman show, but really only so I could play every part and make the rest of the department hate me for my versatility. I always kept a journal that I'd fill with intensely deep sentiments like this:

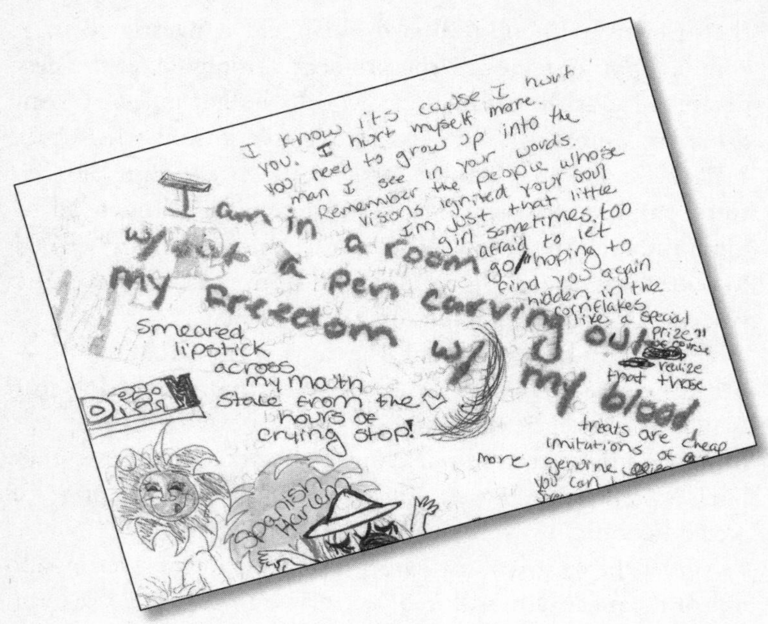

Sometimes I'd contemplate writing a movie, then stop and buy something online instead. I never saw myself as a writer. I have horrible grammar and can't spell to save my life. I never had an English teacher single me out or imply that I showed any promise beyond being a B+ student. If anything, I was japed for my egregious penmanship and misuse of the word "jape." But after hearing "no" enough times, even a B+ student can be pushed to try something new. So I wrote a script.

Unlike acting, I had no expectations. My agents agreed to pass it around, which sounded cool, even though I didn't actually know what "pass it around" meant.

It was a Tuesday night, and Jason and I were over at Amanda and Larry's house for dinner. Larry was busy grilling while Amanda walked around the kitchen, asking if we thought her engagement ring looked small. Just then, my phone rang. I answered the blocked number, assuming it was work related. My manager and agent stopped their conversation and said hello. When both your representatives are on the phone, it's usually a sign that there's good news.

"Good news!" Pamela said cheerfully.

I racked my brain, trying to remember the last thing I auditioned for.

"Am I going to play the mother on *How I Met Your Mother*?"

"Did you audition for that?" my lit agent Leanne asked, confused.

"No. The last thing I went in on was something that involved Highlanders. But I just thought I'd ask. Am I going to play a lady Highlander?"

"No. We actually have some even crazier news." Pamela's line sounded like she'd just walked into Studio 54.

"I'm going to play a man Highlander?"

"No . . . ," Pamela said over the music.

"Wait, where are you?" I asked, straining to hear her.

"My house. Why?"

"Sounds like a party." Leanne shuffled through some papers, half-listening to us.

Pamela had been my manager for over two years, and I always suspected she led a double life. At work, she was a soft-spoken girl with neutral nails and classic style. She rarely cussed, never wore jewelry, and refused to talk about boys. She was almost too appropriate to be real, and because of that I'd convinced myself she was a sex maniac.

Uncomfortable with the attention, Pamela steered the phone call back on track.

"Stan Wylan liked your script and wants to meet you."

The loud thumping of Pamela's Tuesday night sex rave faded away as a door shut behind her. I stopped for a second, collecting my thoughts, then let out a shriek of excitement.

Leanne explained that if I liked and felt I could incorporate Wylan's ideas, we'd work together to develop the script into something he could sell.

"So this meeting is like my final callback?"

"Kind of. Sure." Leanne was still at the office, and I could tell she wanted to get off our call so she could go home to her non-sex-ravey apartment.

"This is awesome. Thank you, guys." I hung up and walked back inside.

Both elated and confused, I explained the situation to Jason.

"A really important person likes my script! He wants to meet me and talk about it."

Saying it out loud felt preposterous. I was never the actress with beginner's luck. I didn't get out of college and accidentally land a starring role opposite Anthony Hopkins.

My first job out of school was a part-time gig making six dollars an hour at the Coffee Bean. Then, after realizing that six times five only equaled thirty, I quit. When the manager called several days later, asking if I wanted my final paycheck, I tried to be nice. "Aw, you can keep it."

My only real goal was to get work as an actress, and that was never easy. Every gig I got felt like a struggle. Then one day, I write a script, mostly just to have something to do with my time instead of feeling sorry for myself, and someone instantly responds. It didn't compute in my mind.

"Why is it that when you don't care about something it comes so much easier? But the things you want more than anything, you rarely get?" I interrupted Jason as he was telling Amanda that she didn't deserve a bigger ring.

"Ew! You aren't my husband!" Amanda stormed away.

"It's like dating," Larry chimed in now, eager to escape the inevitable ring drama. "When someone is too eager to be with you, you assume something is wrong with them. When they kind of don't give a shit, you have to have them."

He was right. With acting, I'd become the needy, desperate carny on the side of the street with three dirty kids and a fiddle. As a writer, I was just an unassuming masochist who knew how to use Final Draft.

I told myself that no matter what happened with Stan Wylan, I was not going to beg, I was not going to cry, and I was not going to buy a fiddle.

The first writer's meeting of my career happened the following Monday. I prepared for it by reminding myself that this whole thing was a fluke and that the outcome didn't matter. I then marched directly into my closet and started stressing out about what to wear, because I obviously needed the outcome to be resoundingly positive and amazing. I tore through my drawers, trying to find the most "writer-y" look I owned. I wanted to make certain I conveyed the proper message: hardworking, lighthearted, but damaged enough to have a good time with. The desperate actor in me settled on all black, allowing Stan and Co. the freedom to project whatever bullshit they wanted onto me.

By Monday, I'd worked myself up so much that I'd started my period two weeks early and a zit I'd almost dried out on my forehead now had a second zit growing out of it. My aesthetician called it a carbuncle. The word alone made me want squeeze the shit out of something, but I refrained and just prayed that Stan's office was dimly lit.

I got to Santa Monica an hour early and parked my car at a thirty-minute meter directly outside. I knew I'd get a ticket, but the thought of driving around the block searching for something better was far too overwhelming.

I walked into a gorgeous, two-story glass building and gave my name to a bitchy, impeccably dressed gay guy whose approval I could already feel myself craving. People always claim that women dress up for other women, but the truth is, women dress up for impeccably dressed gay guys. And this gay guy was *killing it* in a Thom Browne wool-twill mélange two-piece with grosgrain trim throughout and Lanvin brogues.

"I'm Fabian. Have a seat, I'll let Mr. Wylan know you're here," he said, staring directly at the two zits humping on my face.

Before I had time to apply more concealer to my carbuncle, and imagining Fabian scolding me for not owning a Burberry trench, Stan Wylan appeared.

"Hi, Jenny. Come on back."

He was taller than I imagined, with salt and pepper hair and a laid-back, California-kid attitude. Even though he seemed like a charming teddy bear, I knew he had a reputation of being a hard-hitting businessman and even a bit of a bully when things weren't going his way. When we got to his office, he asked me about myself, told me he loved my script, then called in his two development execs, Cosmo and Rico. I tried to relax and prepared myself to agree with anything anyone said.

Cosmo looked ten but was probably closer to thirty. He seemed studious and slightly Aspergers-y. Rico was Latin and loud, and instead of giving me his notes, he found it easier to act them out. I tried to interject lots of head nods, eyebrow squints, and courtesy laughs whenever I could find an opening.

The four of us sat in Stan's pristine, all-white, rich guy office and talked shop for over an hour. Cosmo and I squeezed together on a chenille love seat while Stan and Rico rocked back and forth in matching midcentury Eames bucket chairs. I was intimidated, but felt my performance thus far was golden.

At one point, Cosmo's pen fell from his pocket and landed on Stan's virgin cushions.

"Cosmo, your pen! It just fell out! Don't let that thing bleed all over my couch," Stan cautioned angrily. For a split second, I saw the side of him I never wanted to get on.

Cosmo grabbed the pen, secured the cap, and stuffed it back into his slacks. Besides fearing that Wylan might one day turn on me and eat my face off in an angry rage, I was having the time of my life. For the last decade, the Stan Wylans of the world didn't even know I existed. If they did, it was only as Jason Biggs's wife, who showed up on set and ate all the Zone-Perfect bars. Now I was sitting there as Jenny the Writer. I was being asked for my opinion and acknowledged for my own voice. I felt like I'd stepped into somebody else's life, and I never wanted it to end. Certain I'd lived up to their expectations and grinning from ear-to-ear, I was ready to finally go.

Cosmo and Rico left the room, first giving Stan and me a moment to finish up. Stan continued talking as I gathered my belongings and tried to remain hilarious, competent, and less of a hot mess than the heroine I'd written in my movie.

Then I saw something that made my face go white. I'd say as white as Stan's couch, except it wasn't so white anymore. It was red. Vagina-blood red. Somewhere between Stan telling me he liked my script and me never wanting to give back whoever's life I'd stolen, my period had leaked its way past my super-plus absorbency tampon, through my jeans, and into the fibers of Stan's upholstery. I started to choke on my own breath.

The whole time Stan was worrying about Cosmo's pen going ballistic and ruining his immaculate sofa, I was sitting right next to him, *hemorrhaging all over his goddamn sofa*. As hard as I was trying to be everything they wanted (even though I told myself I wasn't going to do that), the real me was seeping out all over the furniture.

I assessed the situation and deduced that I had only three options: Blame Cosmo the savant, jump out the window (more blood), or confess. I paused to work out the logistics of Cosmo being on the rag when Stan asked if I was okay. Impulsively, I threw my purse over the pancake-sized pool of blood and charged him.

"Stan, listen to me," I said, holding him by both arms against a picture frame collection of him and Adam Sandler doing body shots off each other in Maui.

"I . . . I really don't know how to tell you this and I'm super mortified, but I bled on your couch," I flinched, half-expecting his fist to reach out and deck me in the face.

Stan looked confused and started scanning me for violent wounds. I decided I had no choice but to throw decorum out the window and be completely blunt.

"I got my period all over your couch," I said, settling any doubt in his mind that the crazy main character I'd written into my movie was indeed the real me.

"Umm. Well . . . Don't worry about it," he said, craning his head to see the stain.

Stan wanted me to go, but there was absolutely no way I was going to leave the premises with what looked like a minor miscarriage in his office.

"No, Stan, that's not how this is going to work. I'm staying. You're leaving," I whispered now, calmly revealing the real me.

"What? Where am I going?"

"Anywhere," I said sternly, now pushing him out of the room.

"My assistant Fabian will help you," he offered, acquiescing.

Stan called out to Cosmo and Rico in the adjacent room. "Come on, guys, we're going to lunch."

"Bon appétit!" I waved.

I hovered over the Rorschach test I was about to give Fabian, my could-have-been new gay bestie, and tried to see if the fabric on the couch was by chance a removable slipcover. It wasn't.

"Why are you still here?" Fabian said with one part curiosity, one part "I work for fucking Stan Wylan" arrogance.

"You're not gonna be happy." I laughed nervously. "I . . . Do you have soap, water, sponges . . . ?"

"You spilled your coffee?"

"Not exactly . . ."

"Then what?" Fabian hated me and was about to hate me more.

"Well, actually . . . I'm bleeding."

"From where?" he asked, still not getting it.

"Umm. My pussy." I cut to the chase, scared we weren't moving fast enough.

Fabian looked at the couch, threw up a little in his mouth, then made a beeline for the kitchen. He returned seconds later with a bottle of hand sanitizer.

"I'm not gonna touch you, if that's what you're worried about," I said harshly. I was now over being friends with Fabian, because he was obviously not the type of gay guy who understood women.

"Aren't you a little old to not be in control of your own period?"

I contemplated smearing menstrual blood all over Fabian's

smug little face *Last of the Mohicans*–style, but decided against it, since I did still secretly want him to like me.

After I scrubbed the shit out of the crime scene like a coke-addled Lady Macbeth, Fabian flipped the cushions upside down and returned the cleaning supplies to the kitchen. Looking like I'd just gotten off a shift at the Hormel slaughterhouse, I went to the bathroom to hose myself off. Once the door shut behind me, I lunged into a stall and yanked the saturated tampon out of my body, dropping it into the toilet. My relief lasted only as long as it took me to read the small sign positioned eye level on the back of the stall door:

UNDER NO CIRCUMSTANCES SHOULD YOU EVER
THROW TAMPONS IN THIS TOILET.
WE WILL FIND YOU AND HOLD YOU RESPONSIBLE
FOR THE MASSIVE PLUMBING DAMAGE DONE
AS A RESULT OF YOUR CALLOUS INDISCRETION,
YOU CUNT BITCH.

I couldn't flush my tampon. Stan had an all-male office. If I did, it was going to be so obvious whose period ruined Christmas. Left with no choice, I held my breath, pulled up my left sleeve, and reached into the bowl to fish out my now waterlogged blood baby. Half-drenched in my own urine and the entire production company's DNA, I dropped the 'pon in the trash and fled the scene.

As I walked toward the exit, I could feel the soaking wet sides of my jeans rubbing against my skin. Instantly, I was transported back to my days in theater camp, where I'd laughed at Carly Millhouse when she peed her pants before curtain call. I made a mental note to Facebook-stalk Carly when I got home and write something nice like "Beautiful" on one of her profile pics.

"Everything okay?" Fabian's head was buried in his computer, totally not giving a shit.

"Yes, fine. Thanks again," I said, pretending I wasn't talking to a man who knew the exact color of my menstrual blood.

Just as I got in the car, Leanne called to ask how things went.

"I felt like they had a lot of great ideas, I got my period on the couch, I think most of the changes will be easy to make, I'm gonna reoutline, and let's see . . . I guess that's it!"

The line was dead for a minute, followed by violent coughing. Finally, she responded. "So overall you feel good about it?"

"Umm. Yeah," I said, wondering if she'd heard me correctly.

With the money I'd saved by miraculously not getting a ticket at the thirty-minute meter, even though my car was parked there for two hours over the allotted time, I called Wally's Wines and ordered Stan a basket of pinot noirs. When asked what I wanted the card to say, I paused, really taking in for the first time all that had transpired.

"Just write, 'I got you red to match your couch. XOX, Jenny.'"

Two days later, Stan called, and everything seemed fine. I quickly realized that getting my period on Stan was the best thing that could have happened. After bleeding on someone, there is no point in pretending to be anyone other than yourself. Menstruating really freed me up creatively and allowed me to accept whatever curveballs came my way. I reclaimed my confidence and felt at peace. I ended up working with Stan on the script, with the majority of our meetings over the phone. When I did finally set foot in the office again, everybody including Fabian acted like *it* never happened. When it was time, Fabian gave me the go-ahead to walk back to Stan's office.

Stan was finishing up a phone call when I entered.

"Sit down," he said, motioning toward the crime scene.

I looked over, and covering the white love seat was a giant beach towel. Unsure whether he was joking or serious, I sat on the towel, figuring it was better to be safe than be bloody. Stan hung up, then pulled out his iPhone to take a picture of me.

"You don't care if I put this on my Facebook, do you?"

"Of course not," I lied, wondering if he was by chance friends with Carly Millhouse.

"Your story is now my go-to icebreaker whenever I have meetings in here. It's a huge hit. Everybody wants to know who you are and what you look like. I'm going to frame this picture and put it right next to the couch as a discussion piece."

"Wait, you tell them the story while they are sitting on the bloodstain?" I asked, shocked.

"It's pretty much gone. I had it steam cleaned."

Acting is a total pain in the ass, but writing can be downright disgusting. I did, however, achieve my lifelong goal of making a lasting impression on a big shot producer—at least until he gets a new couch.

Like most scripts, mine probably won't ever see the light of day, but it doesn't matter. As a writer, an "almost" is considered a win. And I am sort of the "baby Judi Dench" of almosts.

If after reading this you are still adamant about pursuing a career in Hollywood, my advice can be summed up in the "secret" I took with me onstage every night as Maria in *The Sound of Music*. "When the Lord closes a door, somewhere he opens a window." Do yourself a favor and jump.

Acknowledgments

Thankfully, most of the people I offended in this book don't read. To those that do, thank you so much for being a part of my life and for coloring the journey so vividly.

Here is a short list of people who deserve a little extra ass-kissing:

Yaniv Soha, my editor, who held my hand through this entire process and only made me cut a few rape jokes. On our first phone call, I said, "You get that I don't know how to write a book, right?" Thank you for teaching me how. I know your parents still don't understand what you do in NYC, but I would just like them to know:

ללא בנכם, ספר זה לא היה
רואה אור. אתם יכולים להיות מאד גאים או כעוסים.
קרוב לוודאי גם וגם.

Liz Brown, who I bamboozled into combing through these stories when she probably should have been writing a funnier book of her own. You make everything better. Groundlings can suck my dick for dropping you one step before company. I can't wait for you to make more money than all of those fucks!

St. Martin's publishers Jen Enderlin (one of my earliest and biggest fans!) and Sally Richardson. The team that so capably supported the promotion of this book: Dori Weintraub, Stephanie Hargadon, Erin Cox, and Angie Giammarino;

John Murphy in publicity, for your early enthusiasm. Cover designer, Jimmy Iacobelli.

Joe Veltre, for getting me this book deal even after certain publishers told you that I should be scolded for the kind of material I put online. Thank you for making my wildest dreams come true.

Priscilla Moralez, for your blood, sweat, and tears. Thank you for never giving up on me and for seeing my path before I did.

Lynn Fimberg, for turning me into a writer.

Jen Craig, for your endless hard work and for not being upset with Lynn for turning me into a writer.

J. J. Harris, one of the absolute greats who unfortunately never got to see this book come to fruition.

The cover photographer and my dear friend Kate Romero; my hair and makeup messiah, Brett Freedman; and the Wizard of Oz who saved me from looking six months pregnant on the cover of this book, Maria Muradyn.

My publicists Leslie Sloane and Jami Kandel, thank you for making me more than just the girl who takes people's iPhone photos with Jason Biggs.

Allyson Ostrowski, Alison Pace, Liz Topp, Peter and Meegan Kiernan, Laura Gibson, Jeff Bailey, Paige Mollen, Brad Mollen, Jaclyn Lessard, Stefan Lessard, Becky Gama-Lobo, Kat Coiro, Derek Richardson, Todd Garner, Jeremy Stein, Sean Robbins, Maurio Garcia, Bobby Hoppey, Nicola Jones, all the girls who attended my sister's bachelorette weekend, David Sullivan, Alice Lawson, Christina Young, Melody Young, my lawyer Chad Christopher and the entire Gersh Agency.

Every actor I've worked with that deserves more attention than they are getting. (You know who you are. The rest of the world doesn't, but you do.)

Melissa Bull at The Smoking Jacket.

Vanessa Butler at Playboy.com.